KOREA
BEYOND THE HILLS

Preceding page: The tranquil waters mirror an early morning ferry as it glides through the misty river, carrying students and farmers. The three rocks called Todamsanbong, rising up in the middle of the river, are one of the eight scenic wonders of central Korea.

KOREA
BEYOND THE HILLS

Photographs and Text by

H. EDWARD KIM

KODANSHA INTERNATIONAL LTD.
Tokyo, New York, San Francisco

Photographs on the following pages © National Geographic Society: 34–35, 38–39, 44–45, 68, 69, 70, 71, 72, 73, 104, 105, 146–47, 174–75.

Distributed in the United States by Kodansha International/USA, Ltd. through Harper & Row, Publishers, Inc., 10 East 53rd Street, New York, New York 10022. In South America by Harper & Row, International Department. In Canada by Fitzhenry & Whiteside Ltd., 150 Lesmill Road, Don Mills, Ontario M3B 2T5. In Mexico & Central America by Harla S.A. de C.V., Apartado 30–546, Mexico 4, D.F. In the United Kingdom by Phaidon Press Ltd., Littlegate House, St. Ebbe's Street, Oxford OX1 1SQ. In Europe by Boxerbooks, Inc., Limmatstrasse 111, 8031 Zurich. In Australia & New Zealand by Book Wise (Australia) Pty. Ltd., 104–8 Sussex Street, Sydney 2000. In the Far East by Toppan Company (S) Pte. Ltd., No. 38 Liu Fang Road, Jurong Town, Singapore 2262. In Korea and for Korean Overseas Organizations by Pan Korea Book Corporation, 134, 1-Ka, Shinmun-Ro, Chongro-Ku, Seoul.

Published by Kodansha International Ltd., 2–12–21 Otowa, Bunkyo-ku, Tokyo 112 and Kodansha International/USA, Ltd., 10 East 53rd Street, New York, New York 10022 and 44 Montgomery Street, San Francisco, California 94104.

LCC 79–91523
ISBN 0–87011–411–5
JBC 0026–787769–2361

First edition, 1980

Kim, Heechoong Edward, 1940-
Korea, beyond the hills.

1. Korea. I. Title.
DS902.K439 951.9 79-91523
ISBN 0-87011-411-5

Book design and layout by H. Edward Kim

CONTENTS

This book is dedicated to

my parents

and those who see

the bare branches of winter

and know they hold the buds of spring

PREFACE

The thrill, the anticipation of coming home that has been building up for months is finally coming to a climax. Out of the airplane window I see the hills—the endless rugged low hills expanding to the horizon, casting shadows like a dragon's back. It is a familiar sight.

Driving from Kimpo Airport through downtown Seoul, my mind won't believe what my eyes see. I am astonished by the tall modern buildings and wide congested city streets, and the new subway system. The country that my heart remembered for the last eighteen years in the United States seems somehow to have leapt forward into a new era.

After the excitement of being introduced to new family members and reunited with boyhood friends is over, I find myself alone in the stillness of the October night. It is the room where I grew up, and my father had kept it just as it was—he knew that I would be back. I look around with much curiosity. There are the old school trophies I had forgotten about and the photographs on the walls, now a little faded. The memories come flooding back, and my curiosity starts to grow. I wonder how much Korea has changed. Are the old customs and traditional values still the same? I know I have certainly grown and changed. They say even the mountains and rivers change in ten years—I wonder if they have.

In this land of ten thousand hills, the lives of rural folk remained sedentary and secure in tradition for centuries. Small farms surrounded by rugged mountains, *yangban* landholders and tenant farmers, pony and ox-cart transportation, Shamanism and ancestor worship have held the people close to the land. Indeed, Koreans have a special appreciation for the beauty of their mountains, streams, and the early morning mists.

Once known as "the Hermit Kingdom," Korea had resisted contact with the Western world as strongly as it had resisted centuries of invaders. But at last, opening its ports to Western traders in the late nineteenth century, Korea began moving into the modern age. The road has not been smooth. Korean social structure was seriously disrupted by the colonial occupation by Japan from 1910 to 1945, and the Korean War further eroded traditional values by bringing the people into contact with foreign troops and previously unknown ways of life. Large numbers of people were uprooted from their ancestral villages as they became refugees.

Since 1960, rapid development has caused agriculture to lose its dominance in the economy to industrial and commercial activities, the urban centers have continued to grow, and the birthrate has declined. A superhighway linking Seoul and Pusan was completed in 1970, the first of many links placing any part of South Korea within a day's driving distance.

Although these ten thousand hills are no longer the barriers that they once were, and traditions are beginning to give way to modern ways, there is still an essence that is the heart of Korea—a national character, a philosophy of life, that is uniquely Korean.

Apart from political preferences or differences, or ideology, it is my goal to share the essence of the Korean people and the land—so much misunderstood in the midst of the national tragedy of the Korean War, the postwar chaos, the search for a new national identity, and the yearning for a unified country. Here is Korea as it is today—a Korea in transition yet unchanging.

Let my house be morning mists,
and my friends the wind and moon;
While the land is at peace
I'll decline into old age.
Just one thing I ask of life:
that my faults may disappear.

—Yi Hwang (1501–70)

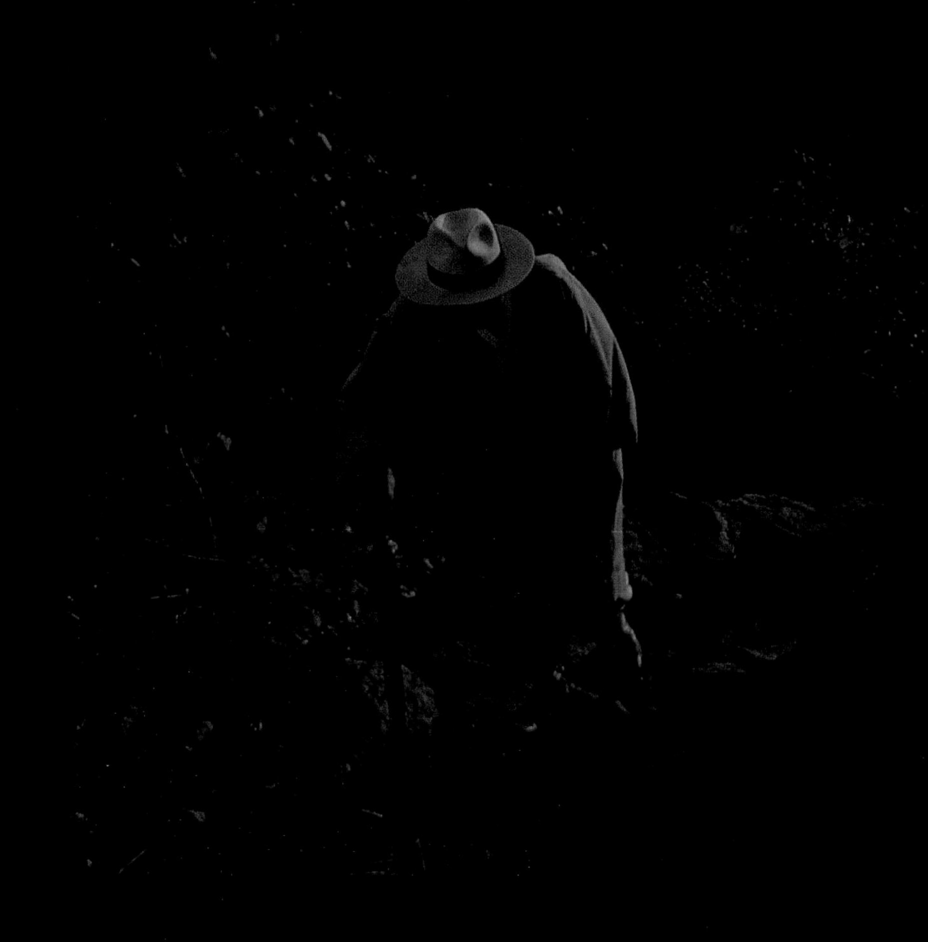

FROM LEGEND TO NEW REPUBLIC

Long ago, in the mists of history and legend, it happened that the wise and brave Heavenly Prince wished to descend from heaven and live among men. His father, the Heavenly King, Lord of Heaven and Earth, granted his wish and provided him with three heavenly seals, three thousand followers, and three ministers: the Lord of the Winds, the Ruler of the Rain, and the Driver of the Clouds. Thus prepared, the Heavenly Prince descended from heaven and appeared under the sacred sandalwood tree on Mt. T'aebaek. He established a great court and ruled wisely, deciding matters of good and evil, and teaching many useful arts such as agriculture and medicine. But all of his followers remained spirits and did not take on human form.

Then one day a she-bear and a tigress who lived in a cave nearby declared that their greatest wish was to become human and walk upon two legs. They prayed so earnestly before the great sandalwood tree that the Heavenly Prince was moved by their sincerity and took pity on them. He gave them each a bunch of mugwort and twenty bulbs of garlic, saying, "Eat these holy foods and hide yourselves in darkness deep in your cave for one hundred days and then you will become human."

So the bear and the tiger ate the food and hid themselves away in their cave. The bear faithfully obeyed all the instructions and curled up to sleep the time away. But the restless tiger could not endure sitting quietly for so long and rushed off on all four legs to go hunting again. Twenty-one days later the patient bear was rewarded. Her hairy coat fell away and she became a beautiful woman.

After a time the bear-woman desired a child. But she could not find a husband, so once again she prayed under the sandalwood tree. The Heavenly Prince heard her prayers and made her his queen. Before long she gave birth to a son who was given the name Tan'gun. Tan'gun established his royal residence at Pyongyang and bestowed the name of Choson upon his kingdom. He brought good ways of living to the land, and after ruling with wisdom for more than one thousand years he flew back up to heaven and became a mountain god.

It is possible that man has been living on the Korean peninsula for more than thirty thousand years. Archeological evidence tells the story of Neolithic life, when large families began the clan structure—groups of families organized by blood relation or by village—that is the basis of Korean society. There are traditions still observed that had their beginnings in these ancient times. The ban against marriage within the same clan, which had the effect of strengthening good relations between clans and promoting the exchange of ideas and technology, remains written law to this day.

The religion of this Neolithic society was based on nature. The spirits that inhabited rocks and trees, rivers and mountains, and controlled events and human fortune, played an important role in daily life. Shamans, who were believed to have special powers over such spirits, conducted ritu-

On National Foundation Day, October 3, thousands of pilgrims climb Mt. Mani on Kanghwa Island before daybreak to honor Tan'gun, the legendary founder of Korea. Facing north, they pay their respects before an altar built by Tan'gun over two thousand years before Christ in honor of his grandfather, the Heavenly King.

als and are still consulted by modern Koreans about family matters, sickness, and even the dedication of new buildings.

Life became much easier with the coming of the Bronze Age in about the eighth century B.C. and the introduction of iron that soon followed. The ruling class had iron weapons; people began to build houses with their new iron tools; and Korea's unique *ondol* floor system for heating was invented. This practical method of heating houses by circulating hot air from a stove through stone-lined flues in the floor is incorporated into modern apartment buildings, although the heat is now provided by electricity or coal instead of wood fires.

Ancient Choson, a predynastic tribal league, established the first kingdom. It was most powerful during the fourth and third centuries B.C., with territory extending from the Taedong River in central North Korea to the Liao River in southern Manchuria. Eventually it was invaded by neighboring China. Korea's boundaries fluctuated through the following centuries as the small peninsula struggled to withstand invasion after invasion. Finally the Yi dynasty established the present border in the fourteenth century A.D., along the Tumen and Yalu rivers that now separate North Korea from the People's Republic of China and the Soviet Union.

Other tribal leagues existed at the same time as Ancient Choson. They grew or declined in power until by the first century A.D. three kingdoms had been founded: Silla and Paekche, which shared the southern tip of the peninsula, and the much larger Koguryo, which reached northward into Manchuria. The formation of these kingdoms brought about a balance of power and stimulated cultural development. Hereditary monarchies were established, social classes appeared, government was centralized, and Buddhism and Confucianism began to be introduced.

Eventually Silla gained control, and the prosperity and power of Unified Silla reached a peak in the middle of the eighth century. The capital, Kyongju, grew to over one million people; many famous Buddhist temples were built, including the beautiful Pulguk-sa temple and Sokkuram Grotto, one of the oldest surviving monasteries in Korea, with its remarkable architecture, wall carvings, and statue of the Buddha so situated that at certain times of the year the first rays of the sun in the morning strike squarely on its forehead.

Korea takes its modern name from the Koryo dynasty, established in A.D. 936 by a rebel leader named Wang Kon. During this dynasty Buddhism enjoyed the protection of the court, and this eventually led to the Buddhist priests gaining excessive power. Confucianism also grew in importance until anyone seeking a government position had to pass an examination on the Confucian classics. The reliance of both of these religions on texts for explication or transmission led to some of Korea's oldest history, folktales, and legends being written down, and to the development of printing. Wooden blocks were used first and then movable metal type, which was invented around A.D. 1234, over two centuries before Gutenberg.

Another great achievement of the Koryo dynasty was the excellence of its celadon pottery. Although celadon with its characteristic pale green glaze was first imported from the Chinese Sung dynasty, Koryo potters soon developed an original technique of inlaid decoration. The Chinese, themselves considered the master potters of Asia, regarded the Koryo celadons as peerless works of art.

Genghis Khan rose to power at the beginning of the thirteenth century, conquering China and harassing Koryo, which remained in a humiliatingly subordinate position to the Mongols for over a hundred years. During this period, while the court was in exile on Kanghwa Island, King Kojong had the text of the Buddhist canon, the Tripitaka, carved on wooden blocks as a gesture of pious patriotism to secure the Buddha's protection against the Mongol invaders. It took sixteen years to complete the 81,258 blocks, and these can still be viewed at Haein-sa temple near Taegu. Declared a National Treasure, they remain the world's oldest and most comprehensive collection of Buddhist scriptures. The end of the Koryo dynasty came in 1392 when General Yi Song-gye seized power, ascended the throne, and moved the capital to Seoul. Thus began the Kingdom of Choson, or the Yi dynasty, that was to last for five centuries.

King Sejong, who came to the throne in 1418, made many valuable contributions to Korean culture and is remembered as the Yi dynasty's greatest monarch. A firm believer in the Confucian doctrine that cultivation of the literary arts leads to individual virtue and therefore virtuous government, King Sejong established a center of learning that conducted political studies and compiled monographs on geography and medicine, official histories, and Confucian commentaries. He also encouraged many scientific advances; on his instructions the lunar calendar was reformed and astrolabes, sundials, water clocks, and rain gauges were devised. White porcelains, lacquer furniture inlaid with mother-of-pearl, paintings, and calligraphy reflect the flourishing fine arts. King Sejong's greatest achievement was probably the invention of the modern phonetic Korean alphabet, called *han'gul*. Realizing how difficult it would be to persuade the Korean people to adopt a new way of writing, he decided that they must have a sign from heaven. So, according to legend, he brushed the shapes of his new letters on fresh green leaves with honey, and then left the leaves in the garden. During the night, earthworms ate their way along the honey trails, leaving behind clear outlines of the letters. Thus King Sejong was able to announce a great miracle. A national holiday now honors this precise alphabet that has only twenty-four letters and is easy to learn.

By the mid-fifteenth century, Korea was being plagued from within by the dissensions of the aristocratic *yangban* landholders, and from without by the Japanese, who wanted free passage through Korea to invade China. Finally, in 1592, Japan's supreme warlord, Hideyoshi, attempted to invade Korea. Seoul fell within two weeks, but the Korean naval forces, under the leadership of Admiral Yi Sun-shin, one of Korea's greatest heroes, inflicted a crushing defeat on the Japanese fleet with the use of "turtle ships," probably the first ironclad ships in history. The Japanese continued their invasion, however, until the death of Hideyoshi; they left behind ruined farms and libraries, a disrupted social system, and an undying hatred of the Japanese. After two more invasions by Manchu armies, Korea retreated into a policy of isolationism and became known as "the Hermit Kingdom."

Western influence slowly began to reach Korea

from China as Jesuit priests and returning Korean envoys brought in foreign maps and books. In 1653 a Dutch ship was wrecked on Cheju Island. One of the survivors, Hendrik Hamel, managed to return to Holland after fifteen years, where he wrote a book about his experiences. Hamel's book provided the first information about Korea, but the Western world paid little attention.

Western religion grew in influence, but its teachings were in direct conflict with Confucian principles, and many missionaries and believers were executed. In 1864 a twelve-year-old boy succeeded to the throne, and his father rose in power as regent. Known as the Taewon-gun, this regent was an orthodox Confucian who opposed change. Two years later when an American merchant ship, the *General Sherman*, attempted to sail up the Taedong River toward Pyongyang, it was burned and sunk with the loss of the entire crew. Korea reluctantly opened its ports to Japan in 1876. A treaty with the United States followed in 1882, and then treaties with Germany, Austria, Russia, Italy, and France. Unfortunately Japan, China, and Russia were involved in a power struggle, and Korea was caught in the middle. Japanese plotting led to the brutal murder of Queen Min in 1895, and the defeat of Russia in the war of 1904–5 placed control of the entire peninsula in Japanese hands. In 1910, the five-hundred-year-old Yi dynasty came to an end: King Sunjong abdicated, and Korea became a Japanese colony.

Japan's clear intent was to exploit the Korean economy, and even before the annexation, Japan had taken over railway concessions, communications, and fishery, timber, and mining rights. The next step was the gradual takeover of land ownership and agriculture, and a great flood of Japanese civilians immigrated to Korea to acquire land and the few skilled jobs that the slowly developing economy generated.

On March 1, 1919, millions of people all over Korea participated in a peaceful demonstration for independence. Throughout the Japanese occupation the Korean people maintained their fierce aspiration that their country be restored to them. Japan reacted with brutality, oppression, and an assimilation policy that attempted to replace the Korean language with Japanese. Korean citizens had to register with the Japanese government under Japanese names, and scenes such as Japanese teachers wearing swords in their classrooms were common.

When the Japanese surrendered to the Allied Powers in 1945, Korea seemed free at last. But the national jubilation was soon overshadowed by the diametrically opposed views of the United States and the Soviet Union over Korea, and the peninsula was divided at the 38th Parallel. Despite the formation of a U.S.–U.S.S.R. Joint Commission and the efforts of the United Nations to set up a commission to advise and consult with the new government, as well as a resolution to hold general elections in Korea to ensure immediate independence and unification, the Russians refused to cooperate and Korea remained divided.

Elections were held in the South under United Nations supervision on May 19, 1948, and the Republic of Korea was officially established. Dr. Syngman Rhee was elected by the Assembly as the first president, and on his inauguration on August 15, exactly three years after Korea's liberation from Japan, the Republic of Korea was proclaimed to the world. The North Korean communists also set up a government: the Democratic People's Republic of Korea, headed by Kim Il-sung.

The Korean War erupted on June 25, 1950. Without warning or declaration of war, North Korean troops crossed the 38th Parallel. Seoul was captured within three days. The United Nations responded by ordering the aggressors to withdraw and encouraging member nations to send aid. The Inchon landing under the command of General MacArthur marked a turning point, and the North Koreans were pushed back to the Yalu River. But Chinese troops intervened, and a stalemate was finally reached, again along the 38th Parallel. Korea is now divided by a neutral Demilitarized Zone, and negotiations at Panmunjom for the reunification of Korea have failed over the last twenty-five years. The Korean War, which lasted for three years until an armistice agreement was concluded on July 27, 1953, devastated the country; millions of people were killed. The suffering and anguish of the Korean people was unparalleled in their history.

The years following the debut of the Republic could hardly be described as good ones. Resources were mismanaged and corruption was widespread. Continued political instability finally forced the autocratic Syngman Rhee to retire. The new rulers turned to the opposite extreme of excessive timidity, and the government of John M. Chang collapsed shortly after being born. Finally, in the spring of 1961, a reform-minded military group led by Park Chung Hee reestablished firm control over the country, executing sweeping reforms, establishing a new progressive tax system, and encouraging business activities. An austerity program was adopted, and certain imports into the country were banned, both to help conserve foreign exchange and to create greater consumption of domestic goods. Price controls were effected, and government releases of farm loans were rapidly made available in large amounts. Park Chung Hee and the military government also created the Economic Planning Board and launched the First Five-Year Economic Development Plan in 1962. This was to prove successful.

Park resigned from the army and was inaugurated into the office of president in 1963. During the next decade, President Park promoted a "new deal" of successive five-year economic development plans that brought rapid industrial and social progress. President Park was assassinated on October 26, 1979, by the former chief of the Korean Central Intelligence Agency, Kim Jae-kyu. The present government, under the leadership of President Choi Kyu Hah, is faced with the challenge of bringing the level of political development up to that of the economy and society at large.

However, the question of unification between North and South remains. Since the Korean War ended in a stalemate in 1953, a shaky truce has prevailed between North and South. The two Koreas face each other at the conference table, but unification is still far off. Despite the constant threat of invasion and the burden that a worldwide recession imposes on the economy, South Koreans face the world with confidence and optimism based on the factors that have kept them one nation and one culture for so long: a clear sense of national identity and a stubborn determination to shape their own destiny.

When I quietly close my eyes, I see
a twisting path across the meadows,
Where the water of the stream

tumbles in runnels in the path,
And under the white poplars
thatched houses hide behind brushwood fences

中華料理

SEOUL: GEOMANCERS' CHOICE

When General Yi Song-gye overthrew the Koryo dynasty, he ascended the throne in 1392 at an old palace in Kaesong. But he soon found that small "Town of the Pines" unsuited to his grand ambitions, so he sent forth geomancers to find the most auspicious site for a new capital. After carefully studying the land's natural features, searching for a place where wind and water could be stored and where the earth's energy was particularly vital and could flow through the crust of the earth to benefit the generations to come, they settled on a small town named Hanyang. This quiet place, half encircled by the Han River, had served as the summer palace for royal families. Surrounded on three sides by mountains and with a fourth mountain facing the royal palace, Hanyang's geomantic conditions were ideal.

General Yi, also known as King Taejo, immediately set about building palaces and a great wall around the city, with battlements, watchtowers, and gates; thousands of laborers were conscripted from the countryside. Legend has it that one night when King Taejo was trying to decide where to build his city wall, it snowed, leaving a circle of white on the hills around the city. Thus the wall was built and the new capital was called Hansong, "the Fortress on the Han." But later the people simply called it Seoul, "the Capital," and so it has been for more than five and a half centuries. Despite centuries of invasions and wars, especially the devastation of the Korean War, when Seoul was lost and regained, and lost and regained, the city has continued to prosper as the nation's capital. Most every Korean has dreamed of visiting it at least once in his lifetime.

The city wall, which was hurriedly built of unshaped stone and clay, has had to be repaired and even rebuilt over the centuries. Once thirteen miles long and twenty to forty feet wide, only portions of it remain as a reminder of times gone by. Of the eight gates that stood on the main points of the compass, only two, the South Gate and the East Gate, are still intact. In the feudal days of the Yi dynasty a great bell was sounded at daybreak to announce the opening of the gates and at sunset to signal their closing. Once the gates were closed, the women, who spent the daylight hours within their homes, were allowed to walk in the city streets. Today the South Gate is surrounded by streams of constant traffic, and the city has sprawled far beyond its original boundaries.

At rush hour the sidewalks and streets are crammed with pedestrians and traffic, shoulder to shoulder and bumper to bumper. The people, smartly dressed in the latest fashions, lend the city the cosmopolitan air of a Paris or a Tokyo. During the day throngs of uniformed schoolchildren fill the parks and palace grounds as their classes take field trips to study art or their nation's history. Even on Sunday mornings the city bustles with large crowds of weekend fishermen and picnicking families waiting at bus stops to head for a day in the country. And Alpiners dressed in

New prosperity draws millions from rural areas, making Seoul one of the ten largest cities in the world. The government is attempting to decentralize the population by creating industrial complexes in rural areas and is contemplating the relocation of the center of government. Seoul's population has mushroomed from 1.5 million in 1949 to almost 8 million today.

leiderhosen eagerly look for the nearest mountain. If there's a parade, better get there early! Crowds line the sidewalks hours ahead of time to be assured of a good spot for watching. In the evenings wine shops open their doors, and the city's entertainment centers come alive with cabarets, theaters, and nightclub revues. Seoul's Broadway is Myung-dong, a thriving shopping area of modern department stores, hotels, theaters, and small shops. Serving native tastes are the huge open markets near the East and South gates, where merchants spread out a vast array of everything from exquisite silk to household items and fresh fish and vegetables.

Seoul, the center of government, education, culture, industry, and entertainment, is truly the heart of Korea. Crowded with almost eight million people, space is naturally at a premium. As old buildings are torn down, they are replaced with wide avenues or even taller structures. The subterranean world is active, too, as shopping arcades are put into tunnels or attached to subway stations. Overpasses enable pedestrians to get across streets filled with heavy traffic, and another level up, elevated expressways cut through the city.

The housing shortage is acute, since many homes were destroyed during the Korean War; this has been aggravated by the great influx of people from rural areas. Seoul constantly struggles to keep pace with the demand. In a few areas of the city, tiled roofs and L-shaped houses still grace the scene, but in numbers they are quickly being outdistanced by more convenient modern apartment buildings. Becoming a modern city brings modern problems, and the ever-increasing number of people and cars and industries has created pollution, which can no longer be ignored. The government is encouraging the creation of new industrial centers in rural areas and is even considering the possibility of moving the political capital.

The presence of the Demilitarized Zone (DMZ) only twenty-six miles away from Seoul and the constant threat of invasion by North Korea make the problem of national security a part of daily life. Tourists can freely visit Panmunjom to see the site of the peace negotiations, but from midnight to 4:00 A.M. a curfew is imposed on Seoul and everyone must remain indoors.

Government buildings are a mirror of twentieth-century struggles. The imposing National Capitol building of marble and granite was built in 1916 on the palace grounds of Kyongbok Goong to house the government under the Japanese regime. It was used by the military government until 1948, by the new government of the Republic of Korea, and then by the Legislative Assembly of the Interim Government. The new National Assembly building is optimistically large enough to hold both the House and the Senate of a unified Korea.

In contrast to the bustle and hubbub of the metropolis and the tension of the DMZ, old palaces and lovely gardens provide islands of quiet and ancient culture in the midst of the city. Kyongbok Palace has suffered many changes since it was built as the residence of the first king of the Yi dynasty, King Taejo. It served as the center of Yi-dynasty power for some two hundred years before being burned down in 1592 by Korean slaves who wanted to destroy the official records of their serfdom. Two hundred and seventy years later, King Kojong became the twenty-fifth ruler of the Yi dynasty, and the palace was rebuilt on the old foundations using the original palace plans. After 1910 all but ten of the five hundred buildings were torn down. Kyongbok Palace is now a beautiful park that provides an appropriate setting for many stone tablets, pagodas, and stone lanterns brought from historic sites throughout Korea for safekeeping. The colorfully painted main throne hall still stands in the middle of a stone-paved courtyard, and an intricately carved thirteen-story marble pagoda of the late Koryo dynasty can be found inside the entrance gate. The National Museum, with its blue-tiled pagoda roof, houses more than eighty thousand priceless art treasures, and villas, pavilions, and lotus ponds give the grounds of "the Palace of Shining Happiness" added charm.

The Changdok Palace has also been rebuilt and renovated over the centuries since it was first built in 1405 as an annex to the Kyongbok Palace. Also called the East Palace, it is the largest and most elaborate of the palaces in Seoul, and it was originally built entirely by joinery techniques without a single nail. It was the residence of the last king of Korea, and the direct descendants of his line still live there. Just north of this palace the Secret Garden spreads out over seventy-eight acres of hills and clear ponds and streams. Bridges, pavilions, huge old trees, and narrow pathways keep the secrets of the past, but Seoulites and tourists now enjoy its restful beauty, as well as a zoo and botanical gardens nearby.

The third major palace in Seoul is Toksu, "the Palace of Virtuous Longevity," which was not intended to be a palace at all. After the Japanese invaders were turned back in the sixteenth century, all the palaces were in ruins, so King Sonjo moved into Toksu temporarily; it has been a royal palace ever since. With its mixture of Western and Oriental, old and new architectural styles, it can be viewed as a symbol of Seoul. A Renaissance-style building built early in the twentieth century now houses the Museum of Modern Art.

Every year Confucian ceremonies are held at Chongmyo, the Royal Ancestor's Shrine, which was built in 1395 by King Taejo to memorialize his ancestors. Since then the ancestral tablets of the kings and queens who followed him were added to the shrine through the centuries, including those of the last king, King Sunjong. Today the members of the former royal family still attend the annual services, conducted with colorful pomp and ritual on the first Sunday in May.

The palaces and shrines of Seoul reflect the cultural heritage and glory of the past, but Seoul's universities and training schools are creating the technology and leaders of the future. Well over half of the university students in the country are concentrated in the city. And the four major universities, Seoul National University, the Korea University, Yonsei University, and Ewha Women's University, all located in Seoul, are well known as the elite schools whose graduates are to be found in leadership roles in government and business.

As the capital of a newly industrialized nation, Seoul has taken on a boomtown atmosphere. Circulating 20 percent of the nation's currency, the city also boasts 25 percent of Korea's manufacturing, 45 percent of its motor vehicles, and 60 percent of its hospitals. With its industry and museums, palaces and universities, Seoul embodies the spirit of the past and the spirit of a new age.

A panoramic view of downtown Seoul jammed with hotels and office buildings. Despite centuries of invasions and the devastation of the Korean War, the city has continued to

prosper as the capital of a newly industrialized nation growing at an unprecedented rate and as the hub of Asia's fastest growing economy during most of the 1970s.

It's a parade! Marching bands and colorful confetti mark National Armed Forces Day. The military academy cadets marching through city hall square and cheering schoolgirls with balloons and flags celebrate the strength of Korea's armed forces.

With the Demilitarized Zone separating North and South only twenty-six miles away from Seoul, national security is of utmost concern to every citizen. The effort to unify the country through negotiation has thus far been unsuccessful, and peace between the two sides remains in a delicate balance.

In the evening hours streets fill with Seoulites heading for home, and street vendors at the bus stops add color to the busy scene. The city, surrounded by mountains and once ringed by a thirteen-mile wall with eight gates, has been sprawling outside of its enclosure. As evening falls, families gather around television sets to enjoy their favorite serialized dramas; wine shops open on the back streets; and the shopping districts come alive with bustling crowds. All business must end by midnight, as a 12:00 to 4:00 A.M. curfew is imposed on the city for national security.

30
週刊京鄕

The charm of a once small city disappears under the façade of Westernization. The huge districts situated south of

the Han River are studded with new highrises to accommodate ever-growing numbers of inhabitants.

Bursting at the seams and creating a boomtown atmosphere, city streets and elevated expressways are regularly clogged with traffic. With 33,000 persons per square mile and projections that the city's population in ten years will exceed Tokyo's, Seoul is experiencing acute growing pains.

To ease the traffic, construction of the eighty-six-mile subway system is in full swing, twenty-four hours a day, to complete it by 1983, two years earlier than planned. Until then the city's 5,500 buses are the primary means of transportation, moving an estimated 4.7 million people daily.

정 진
55

A fantasy of women's fashion. Aesthetic creations of designer André Kim are

reflected on the faces of film star Chang Mi-hee, at right, and model Jean Won-ki.

At the great East Gate market, shoppers can find an abundance of everything from colorful silk to myriad piles of fresh vegetables, dried fish, and ginkgo nuts. Although supermarkets and department stores offer convenient modern shopping, housewives and bargain hunters enjoy the open marketplace.
Following page: Overshadowed by highrise apartment buildings, the graceful wingtipped tiled roofs of the traditional L-shaped houses are perhaps the last vestige of old-style living. The scarcity of land and the convenience of apartment living are contributing to the rapid disappearance of these once preferred houses.

Their faces as soft as the color of turning leaves, young girls escape the hectic pace of the city in the Secret Garden of Changdok Palace. When the crimson maple leaves decorate the city parks, the Secret Garden is a favorite place to visit. During the Yi dynasty, the lovely garden with its pavilions and pagodas and ponds and streams scattered over seventy-eight acres of hills was reserved for the pleasure of the royal family and palace women.

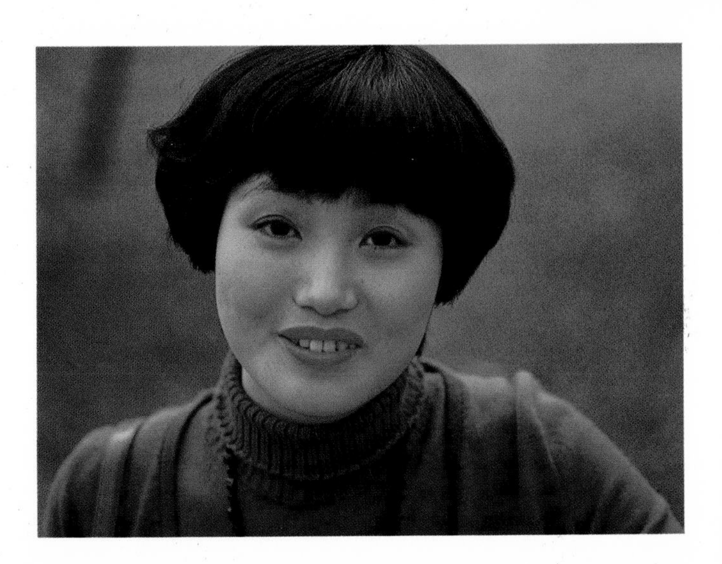

Simple weekend pleasures. Families gather in Namsan Park to exercise in the fresh clear morning air. Physical fitness is enjoying increasing popularity, and many families are taking up calisthenics, jogging, and tennis.

Amateur photographers focus on a model posed in front of the National Museum with its five-tiered pagoda top. Photo clubs and photography businesses often sponsor contests using well-known models and movie stars, drawing hundreds of eager camera buffs. *Following page*: Early morning fog blankets Chongnung, the tomb of Queen Sindok, who was the second wife of King Taejo, founder of the Yi dynasty. Much of the charm of this bustling, vibrant city lies within the walls of colorful palaces and parklike royal tombs.

The Great String of the Black
Lute sounds
as I move the goosefoot along,
Like water that was icebound
bursting booming into the
stream.
Now I hear raindrops falling on
lotus leaves:
are they trying to match this
music?

—Chong Ch'ol (1536–93)

東白軒

LIVING TREASURES AND FOLK ARTS

Gifts and talents that are carried in the minds and hearts and skillful fingers of craftsmen and artisans, dancers and musicians, represent a cultural heritage that cannot be put in a museum or protected like a historic site. The Living Treasures of Korea are people with skills that have been handed down through generations among the common people, or protected by the patronage of the royal court.

Since Korean life has been disrupted so greatly in recent decades by the colonial rule of Japan, the postliberation turmoil, the Korean War, and tremendous socioeconomic changes, it is a wonder that folk culture has survived at all. The Korean people struggled throughout the Japanese occupation to retain a sense of identity, yet gradually intangible cultural assets began to be neglected. For example, Korean court music was simply not used after the last royal dynasty was abolished in 1910, and there is little purpose in laboriously weaving by hand when fabric can be easily purchased.

Since the early 1960s, increasing economic growth and political stability have fostered an awareness that these cultural assets must be protected to prevent their total disappearance. The Ministry of Culture and Information with the Cultural Property Preservation Bureau seeks to search out and appraise intangible assets and give them official recognition and protection. The first task is to record the form, nature, and method of each asset, then to ensure the training of apprentices and others who will carry on the craft or art, and finally to offer financial support and opportunities for public exhibitions or performances. Drama, dance, music, and crafts that are considered part of the cultural heritage are now preserved for all to enjoy.

Many of the people who have been designated by the government as Living Treasures have been practicing their crafts since their youth and are now in their retirement years. Others are younger artists who devote all their time to the creation of new work based on the traditional methods. Museums, universities, and private endeavors like the Korean Folk Village near Suwon south of Seoul provide opportunities for displaying, learning, and observing the ancient crafts. Horsehair hat making, metalworking, weaving, bamboo craft, and pottery are just a few of the crafts now protected by the government.

Pottery has been a part of Korean life since late Neolithic times, around 3000 B.C., and each dynasty has left behind superb examples of this art form. Silla stoneware resembles many contemporary Chinese specimens and uses incised geometric designs. But the celadons of the Koryo dynasty are stunningly original in both decoration and technique. Ranging from bluish green to pale brown, these stoneware-bodied pieces are often lobe-shaped—resembling gourds or melons—and show a great diversity of floral patterns. Their most distinguishing feature is the use of inlaid decoration beneath the glaze, a Korean invention. Yi-dynasty porcelain is noted

With a smile as bright as her costume, a sixth grader participates in the Farmer's Dance with her classmates in the National Annual Folk Dance Contest.

The Farmer's Dance is one of the most popular and widely known of all Korean dances. Once performed by farmers on festival occasions, it is disappearing from the rural scene. To preserve such cultural assets, a few schools now offer afterschool classes.

for its outstanding brushwork and design. The excellence of Korean pottery was recognized throughout Asia, and at various periods of history the Japanese even captured and moved whole villages of Korean potters to Japan. The potters taken during Hideyoshi's invasion in 1592 were put to work making tea-ceremony wares and later helped establish the Japanese porcelain industry.

Also outstanding for their quality and level of artistry are Korean bronze bells. The oldest existing bells are from Buddhist temples of the Unified Silla period in the eighth century. The largest is the Emille Bell, eleven feet high and weighing approximately twenty tons. It is said that it can be heard forty miles away on a clear night. Unfortunately the ancient techniques for casting such large bells have been lost, although perhaps through modern research they can be recreated.

Korean court music played by an orchestra equipped with ancient drums, gongs, and lutes, and dressed in brilliant court musicians' costumes, is as exciting to watch as it is to hear. Some of the instruments are of Korean invention, such as the *komun-go*, a long six-stringed zither that dates back to the Koguryo period in the seventh century A.D. The popular Korean hourglass drum, or *chang-go*, is used for a wide variety of music, from orchestral productions and poetry reading to folk dancing. It has two heads and can produce both a deep tone and a sharper sound. Bronze bells and jade chimes are hung chromatically in two rows on large decorative wooden frames. The bronze bells are louder and used more often in outdoor ceremonies, Confucian rites, and Chinese-style music. Other instruments include gongs, lutes, flutes, and multiple-reed oboelike pipes. Instead of being thought of as percussion or wind instruments, these ancient Korean instruments are categorized by the materials they are made from, such as metal, stone, silk, bamboo, gourd, clay, leather, or wood.

We know what early Korean music was like thanks to King Sejong in the fifteenth century. The king was an avid promoter of all forms of Korean culture, and it was his interest that led to the music of the time being codified and rearranged. Although this Yi-dynasty music was primarily based on the music and dance of the Koryo period, and no new original forms were added, the preservation of the scores in written form was a major achievement; not only court music, but folk songs and love songs were written down for the first time. The royal court orchestra was abolished after 1910, but between then and the organization of the National Classical Music Institute in 1945, all the old books, manuscripts, and notated music were carefully saved.

The variety of court music that can thus be heard today includes the ancient Chinese music that was performed in Confucian rituals, the court music that had its origins in Tang China, and country music performed for dancing that dates from the fifth century A.D. Military music was played by two bands: a louder band with brass instruments and gongs marched in front of an important personage such as the king, and a softer ensemble with flutes followed behind. Chamber music, dance music, lyric songs, storytelling songs, and *sijo* can all still be performed authentically. *Sijo*, dating from the Koryo period, is perhaps the most representative form of Korean poetry and is still written today. Dealing with ethics, love, and nature, a *sijo* is composed of three units, or lines, whose syllables (never more than forty-five in all) follow a conventional arrangement. It is considered primarily a literary form, although the authentic *sijo* was meant to be slowly chanted or sung to the accompaniment of the hourglass drum.

The lively art of dancing has had a place in Korean life since the seasonal celebrations at planting and harvest in ancient times before Christ. Although there are few written records, two important works on music and dance have survived from the Yi dynasty and contain detailed descriptions as well as a history of dance in Korea since the Silla dynasty. Tomb paintings of the fourth to sixth centuries from the Koguryo period also exist, depicting dancers and musicians. Many of these old dances have been designated as intangible cultural assets in order to protect them.

Confucianism, Buddhism, and Shamanism had an influence on both music and dance since they were important elements in religious rituals. The Confucian Line Dance, in which one person dances while balancing himself on a rope strung between two poles, is still performed at the annual rites before the Yi-dynasty ancestral tablets and at the spring and fall festivals at the Confucian Shrine in Seoul. Buddhist dances came to Korea from India through China over seventeen hundred years ago, but they retain no trace of their Indian origins. Preserved by a small sect of monks, these dances, such as the Drum Dance, the Cymbal Dance, and the Butterfly Dance, are performed to attract attention to the Buddhist ceremony and are no longer supplications to the Buddha as originally intended. Shamanistic rituals use loud music and frenzied dancing to exorcise evil spirits or bring good luck. Dating back to the time of nature worship, these rituals are full of exuberant high spirits and can sometimes go on for days.

Court dances were presented at banquets for the entertainment of the royal court. The carefully and exactly prescribed movements are slow and graceful to display the dancers' rich and beautiful appearance. Folk dances, on the other hand, are free and creative. The Farmer's Dance is one of the most popular of these. Wearing brilliant red and blue and green sashes and vests over white clothes, the performers improvise intricate movements to the raucous music of the farmers' band. Long white paper streamers attached to the tops of the dancers' hats are looped and twirled in great figure eights, creating quite an exciting spectacle.

As colorful as the dancers' costumes, *minhwa*, "the people's art," brings protection and good luck through gaily colored paintings pasted over doorways in Korean homes. This folk art, portraying everyday life and an impressionistic view of nature, has its roots in Shamanistic beliefs. Paintings of animals such as tigers and roosters guarded front entrances from evil spirits, and others depicting symbols of learning such as books and brushes were often found in the homes of those for whom education could only be a dream.

Amateurs and court painters created most of these paintings, leaving their work unsigned. Their bold and sometimes comical work was a part of daily life and received little attention as an art form. In recent years, as the standard of living has risen, people are taking pride in their cultural heritage and rediscovering the charm of this Korean folk art.

ORNAMENTAL KNOT & CORD

Designated National Living Treasure #22, Kim Hee-jin weaves a pattern into a silken cord. From raw silk thread to completed work of art, Kim, forty-five, creates her own designs based on her knowledge of the traditional art. She uses plant dyes to obtain the desired colors before she weaves the intricate cord into ever more elaborate knots. Her concentration is so intense that she sometimes has to rest in bed for a few days after completing a piece of work.

This ancient art came to Korea from China, possibly during the Three Kingdoms period, and became very popular during the Yi dynasty. The beauty of each piece lies in the combination of cord, knot, and tassel. A perfect knot is symmetrical and identical on front and back. After the cord is intertwined it is carefully and evenly tightened. Individual knots and tassels have poetic names such as the Chrysanthemum and Dragonfly knots, and the Strawberry, Phoenix, and Octopus tassels.

FLOWER SILK SHOES

Born in 1889, Fwang Han-gop practices the art of making flower shoes—the decorated leather shoes that were once worn by the royal families and noblemen of the Yi dynasty. The queens and ladies of the court wore similar shoes, made of silk and leather but more richly embroidered with flowers.

Although Fwang never received a formal education, he learned the craft in his boyhood. His exceptional skill has earned him recognition as National Living Treasure #37.

Today mass-produced rubber shoes have replaced the traditional leather footwear, and Fwang's flower shoes are made for display and special occasions. His grandson is a serious apprentice and hopes to carry on the art.

PATTERNS OF TEMPLE PAINTING

Rainbow hues decorate temple eaves. As a young boy of fourteen, Won Dukmoon entered the Buddhist priesthood and learned the technique of temple painting. Having traveled all over Korea and studied art in Japan, he is devoting his life to temple paintings. Won, aged sixty-six, is now National Living Treasure #48 and spends much of his time restoring paintings for old temples. His latest work is a painting of a white-bearded mountain god accompanied by a tiger, a popular subject of Korean beliefs.

THE MASTER OF LACQUERWARE

National Living Treasure #10, Kim Bong-yong is a master of lacquerware. Some fifty years ago, as a sixteen-year-old apprentice, he learned the unique method of inlaying mother-of-pearl from old masters.

The production of lacquerware in Korea dates back to the fourth or fifth century B.C., and although lacquered objects originally came from China, mother-of-pearl inlaid designs are a Korean addition. Some of the most popular motifs are plum branches, bamboo, flowers, birds, landscapes, and animals such as the crane or turtle that symbolize longevity.

Preceding page: At the Korean Folk Village near Seoul, a man demonstrates basket weaving, once considered one of the lowliest professions.
This page: People of Dam-Yang village, known for its abundant bamboo, weave baskets to supplement their farming income. Slicing the bamboo into thin strips requires special skill, and it takes many months of practice to become a competent basket weaver. In the past, bamboo baskets were an important household item, and the basket maker was a common sight in the village marketplace. But nowadays people use molded plastic containers, and many of the delicate works of bamboo are exported.

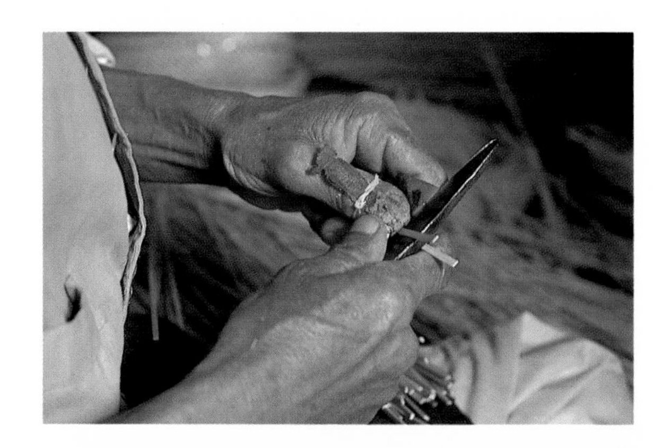

Traditional dances have been strongly influenced by Buddhism and Confucianism. The comic Mask Dance-Drama satirizes the privileged social classes—the *yangban* nobility and Buddhist priests—while the Monk's Dance expresses the agony of priesthood. The Court Dance reflects the grandeur and propriety of Confucian rites.

Played by the royal orchestra before 1910, Korean court music is now preserved and performed by the National Classical Music Institute. Wearing the brilliant traditional court musicians' dress, the orchestra presents a variety of music such as Confucian ritual music, court music that originated in Tang China, chamber music, and dance music. Both five- and seven-note scales are used.

Instruments include the *komun-go* (*opposite*), an original Korean zither with six strings that dates back to the Koguryo period, as well as a large bamboo flute (*above*) and bronze bells, gongs, jade chimes, lutes, multiple-reed pipes, and drums.

TREASURES FROM THE PAST

The romance and excitement of opening a royal tomb or diving for treasures shipwrecked and buried in the sea for centuries have recently created a new awareness of the vast richness of Korea's artistic heritage. Every age and aspect of Korean society seem to have been touched in some way by the variety and beauty of artistic expression. The works that have come down to us today share a spontaneity and simplicity that can only have come from the confident vitality of the craftsmen who made them. Cone-shaped pottery jars decorated with comblike herringbone patterns served as vessels for Neolithic man; ornate gold crowns, belts, and jewelry show the strength of Shamanistic beliefs in sixth-century Silla; exquisite celadons with their underglaze designs of Korean invention were the prized possessions of Yi-dynasty royalty and have been an inspiration to potters around the world. As centuries passed, the influences of China, Taoism, Buddhism, and Confucianism shifted and changed, while the animistic expression of Shamanism was an underlying constant. This mix of cultures can be seen in the way Korean art blends humor, boldness, vigor, and a strong and joyous love of nature.

Left: Small holes show that this twelfth-century Koryo monkey and baby was used as a water dropper. The expression of the mother and the baby's affectionate gesture, touching its mother's face, are realistic and alive although the potter must have used a painting as a model since there were no monkeys in Korea, at least during recorded history.

Right: This solid gold Amitabha, or Buddha of the Western Paradise, was found in a bronze box in the second story of a stone pagoda near the Silla capital of Kyongju. According to the inscription on the cover of the box, the image was offered by King Songdok in A.D. 706 in memory of the previous king.

The facial type and drapery folds, falling over the throne, indicate that the statue may have been copied after a Tang model, but the human amiability and spiritual purity were characteristic of Korean Buddhistic sculpture until the eighth century.

This noble warrior on horseback was discovered in a tomb near Kyongju in 1924. He may well represent the master of the tomb on his journey to heaven, attired in the formal dress of a Silla noble. Made during the fifth or sixth century A.D. this stoneware vessel is an example of the sophistication and humor of Silla potters. *Above*: Who the painter of this tiger was is not certain, but he is generally believed to be Sim Sa-jong, a well-known painter of the eighteenth century. The poem at the top of the scroll reads:

The ferocious tiger with grinding teeth
Who would dare to confront it?
Grievous times bring forth the old yellow lord
Of the Eastern Seas.
Who recognizes today among the swaggerers
And the perverse these same tigers?

Regarded as one of the best of its type, this seventeenth-century white porcelain vase, with grapevine tendrils stretching out across its bulging shoulder in an underglaze iron design, is representative of those produced at the central government kiln. Ceramic ware of the Yi dynasty is characterized by spontaneity and naiveness in basic approach and a tendency to minimize the decorated area.

Right: A renowned Neo-Confucian scholar and painter of the Yi dynasty, Yi Jae entered government service and held several high positions before retiring at age forty-seven to teach Confucian philosophy. His portrait, by an anonymous artist, conveys the dignity and intelligence of the old scholar as well as his uncompromising sternness. Officials, as an expression of nationalism, often had their portraits painted in simple white Korean dress instead of the ornate Chinese-style court robes.

The day-star's set, the larks are in the sky.
Shouldering a hoe I leave my yard.
There is heavy dew in the woods,

my hempen shorts are soon soaked.
Come now, lad, when times are good,
does it matter if your clothes get wet?

—Yi Chae (1725–76)

VIEW FROM THE HILLS

Before the morning sun wakes the farmers, the sound of roosters crowing echoes through the valley. Smoke begins to rise from the chimneys of the tiny farmhouses with tiled roofs, clustered together at the foot of low green hills. Steaming rice and soup soon appear on the breakfast table. A man on a bicycle with a young girl in a school uniform riding behind appears on the tree-lined road, winding through harvested rice fields under the crystal clear blue sky of autumn.

As the sun rises higher in the sky a woman starts out for the fields, carrying a basket of lunch on her head, followed by a child with an aluminum tea kettle full of rice wine. The thrumming of the rice threshing machine comes to a halt when the farmers stop for their noonday meal. Sitting in a circle around the lunch basket, they talk about the rising cost of fertilizer and seeds, the price their harvest will bring, and their children returning from faraway cities for the holiday.

Evening brings the distant tinkle of cow bells, farmers returning from the field, and children running about the courtyards filled with red peppers spread out in the sun to dry. The orange sky slowly fades as darkness falls. Only the faint outline of the hills surrounding the valley remains. These tranquil scenes of the countryside are remembered as home by many Koreans.

With clear skies and high mountains, small villages nestled against the hillsides and emerald green rice paddies in the spring, cosmopolitan cities and bustling seaports—all in a space the size of Iceland or Portugal—South Korea is a nation of amazing contrasts. Its land and all its resources must provide for a population of thirty-seven million people, yet only one-fourth of the land can be cultivated. Carved and terraced into paddies, little pockets of green and gold dot the valleys and hillsides in spring and fall.

Traditionally, farming has been a hard and near-subsistence way of life. Farms have always been small, usually less than three acres, and divided into many small plots, making the use of most kinds of machinery impractical. In the past, poor rocky soil, the lack of chemical fertilizers, and insufficient irrigation caused many farmers to endure continuing hardship while a few landholders of the *yangban* ruling class enjoyed prosperity. Tenant farmers, who were in the majority, were often on the brink of starvation after paying the exorbitant rents demanded by the *yangban*. Every spring when last year's harvest had been depleted, times were especially hard. The weather also caused great difficulties. Although there was generally sufficient rainfall, the climate did not allow for more than one crop a year, and drought or heavy rains could cause much damage.

Today the Korean countryside wears a new look: concrete blocks and tile roofs have replaced the old thatch-roofed houses with their walls of stone and clay; small tractors and tillers are seen more often than wooden ox-drawn plows; and an experimental rice-transplanting machine appears occasionally. Although there is naturally a nostalgia about the passing of the old ways, the changes have brought an easier way of life.

A Korean Gothic. As the evening sun brushes the terraced field with a golden hue, a man and wife, with towels on their heads and sickles in hand, pause for a moment in their long day's work. At this hectic time of year they rush to harvest their late-spring wheat while rice seedlings wait to be transplanted.

New farming methods have greatly increased the productivity of Korea's small farms. Irrigation and chemical fertilizers, the use of machinery and double cropping, cash crops and cooperative seed beds, and cross-breeding to produce more resistant grains with higher yields have all contributed to this agricultural success story. In fact the rural income is now competitive with that in urban areas, and the countryside is a most attractive place to be, with its improved living conditions, fresh clean air, and serene landscape.

The New Community Movement, or Saemaul Undong, was initiated by President Park Chung Hee in 1971. It has brought about many positive changes and has been largely successful in its goal of eliminating rural poverty. Through this government-sponsored program, farmers have been able to improve their homes with new floors and plumbing and to purchase farming equipment with low-interest loans. Villagers have also learned how to use their own resources, and with government aid toward the purchase of building supplies, such as concrete, have built community meeting halls and local roads, and made many other improvements that have raised the quality of village life.

Traditionally, farmers used to spend the winter months catching up on domestic chores, making straw shoes and baskets and rope, while their children played on the frozen rice fields. The New Community Movement encourages them to establish small rural industries and raise pigs and winter vegetables in order to increase cash income and make the bitter cold months more profitable.

The Saemaul Undong spirit of diligence and cooperation has become a national effort, touching the lives of city and country dwellers alike. In the spring, especially if there has been a drought, when the paddies fill with water and the rice seedlings must quickly be transplanted, and in the fall when crops must be harvested as fast as possible before it rains, everyone helps out.

All over Korea rice paddies reflect the seasons as they stand empty in the winter, are brilliantly green in the early summer, and turn gold in the fall. More than a third of the cultivated land is devoted to rice, and a farmer may expect to make half of his income from it. In early spring the paddies are fertilized and plowed and raked, and the best are planted as seed beds. When the rice seedlings are ready in May they are transplanted to the waiting wet rice fields—a task that takes weeks of back-breaking labor. During the summer the rice fields are cultivated and weeded by hand, and compost is prepared for next year's crop. In September the golden rice is harvested, bundled, dried in the sun, and threshed.

Rice is such an important part of Korean life that it even used to be a symbol of social status: a man who ate rice three times a day was well off, while a poorer person had to mix his rice with beans or barley, and a peasant woman might only get a bowl of rice on New Year's Day and her birthday. Holiday rice cakes with red beans, rice wine, cakes, cookies, and dumplings are just a few of the many ways this staple is used. Other grains include wheat, barley, soybeans, and corn; fruits and vegetables, however, are becoming increasingly important crops.

The city of Taegu has become the apple capital of Korea since apples were first introduced by a missionary around the turn of the century. And anyone who has tasted sweet, crisp, juicy Korean pears that are big and green and shaped like apples will proclaim them the best in the world. Oranges, tangerines, and pineapples are only grown on Cheju Island, where the tropical climate is ideal for citrus fruit. Walnuts, chestnuts, and pine nuts are indigenous to Korea, and the chestnut vendor is a common sight in the city, selling hot roasted chestnuts to warm both the hands and stomach on cold winter days.

Korea's most widely known crop is ginseng; it has been exported from Korea for more than fifteen hundred years and is valued for its quality and curative properties. Most of it is grown on Kanghwa Island near Seoul where rows and rows of thatched-straw sheds protect the tender plants from the elements. It takes six years to bring a crop to maturity, so harvest time is a great occasion. After the roots are dug up they are washed and then dried or steamed. Said to cure ailments and promote energy, ginseng has been treasured more than gold; the discovery of wild plants in the mountains could mean a fortune.

Spicy hot *kimch'i* is the most famous of all Korean dishes. Made of pickled Chinese cabbage and other vegetables such as cucumbers, turnips, and radishes and seasoned with ginger, salt, and hot red pepper, it is packed into large earthenware jars and left to ferment. A method of preserving vegetables through the winter, *kimch'i* comes in countless varieties, and each fall in October families buy literally truckloads of vegetables to make their winter supply.

Another Korean favorite is the persimmon. In October when the air is crisp and clear and the leaves have begun to fall off the trees, bright red-orange persimmons can be seen hanging against the clear blue sky. After they have been touched by the first frost they are sweet and juicy, and some are dried at this stage to be enjoyed through the winter. But beware to the person who attempts to eat a persimmon that is not yet ripe! Its bitter taste is strong enough to frighten a tiger; but its ripe sweetness can soothe a crying child, as in this comical old folk tale:

One dark night a tiger came creeping stealthily into a mountain village. There was the sound of a child crying and he stopped to listen. He heard the mother's voice scolding and threatening, "If you don't stop crying a tiger will come and get you!" But the child just kept on crying and crying. "My! My!" the tiger thought. "Not afraid of me? This child must be very brave indeed!"

Then he heard the mother say, "Here's a persimmon." And immediately the child stopped crying. "Oh!" the frightened tiger said to himself. "This persimmon must be a fierce and terrible creature!"

Thus he gave up the idea of eating the child for dinner, and off he went looking for an ox to feast on instead. Quietly he crept into a shed. Unbeknownst to the tiger, a thief was already there intending to steal the ox, and in the darkness the thief mistook the tiger for the ox and jumped on his back.

The tiger was simply terrified and ran off into the night as fast as he could go, yelling, "Help! Help! A terrible persimmon is attacking me!" And all the while the thief was on his back urging him to go faster and faster so he could get away before the villagers caught him stealing the ox.

When it grew light the thief was astonished to see that he was riding on a tiger and quickly jumped off. But the tiger just kept on running and never looked back.

A man returning home from gathering firewood in the hills, palely silhouetted in the distance behind a line of poplar trees, was once a common sight in rural Korea. His huge bundle of branches for kindling is tied onto an A-frame *jiggeh*.

As late as the turn of the century Korea was covered with dense forests where tigers used to roam, but reckless overuse soon denuded the hills. The use of charcoal briquettes and serious reforestation programs are beginning to cover the hills with green.

Reputed to cure ailments from fatigue to hangovers and to improve anything from blood circulation to sex drive, ginseng is known worldwide as the "elixir of life." Taking its name from the Chinese character for "man," the root is said to resemble the human figure. It takes six years of careful, patient care to bring a crop to maturity, and thatched-straw roofs are used to protect the tender plants from too much wind and rain and sun.

Perched high in the branches, a Buddhist monk picks ripe persimmons using a long bamboo pole with a forked end. His companion below catches the luscious fruit as it is thrown down from the tree. The fruits of fall, walnuts and persimmons, are prepared for a valued guest visiting this remote mountain temple. Usually harvested after the first frost of autumn, ripe persimmons are sweet and juicy. If picked too soon, they are bitter and cause an unpleasant and unforgettable puckering of the mouth!

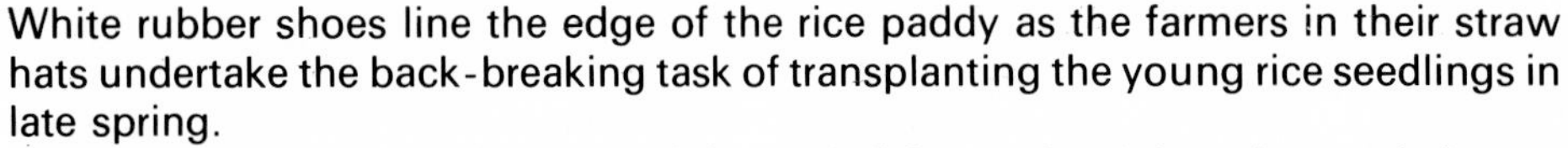

White rubber shoes line the edge of the rice paddy as the farmers in their straw hats undertake the back-breaking task of transplanting the young rice seedlings in late spring.

Rice-harvest time begins toward the end of September when the maple leaves turn red and gold. Gasoline-powered threshing machines thrum in the countryside as they separate the bundles of rice into grain and straw. The straw will be used to make such items as hats and bags and rope. In the peak of the season families combine their efforts to help each other gather their harvests.

A family pauses for a midday snack of steamed sweet potatoes and a bowl of rice wine. The farmer takes this opportunity to resharpen his L-shaped hand sickle, or *nat*, with a whetstone. The A-frame *jiggeh* standing nearby is convenient for carrying their lunch and tools. During the busy harvest the entire family is needed in the field, and the small children play or nap close by.

They watch with wonderment as an express bus whizzes by on the cosmos-lined country highway.

The hills are higher in the east. Although the beauty of the rugged mountain ranges is much admired, life among these hills has been hard. As this woman picks beans in her backyard garden, her weathered face reflects the hardships of life in the mountains.

The small farms wedged into the narrow mountain valleys are only suitable for growing vegetables, and farmers hunt the steep and rocky mountainsides for medicinal herbs and roots, and trap small wild animals.

The high hills are no longer the barriers they once were to these mountain villages. Improved roads alleviate the isolation of these remote areas and new methods of farming help raise the standard of living.

Domestic chores and tending cows fill the days of the village grandfather. In the Korean families of past generations, the grandfather had the responsibility of running the household, which gave him a useful role and a strong sense of security.

As evening nears, a woman returning from market with her purchases on her head manages to give her child a ride.

Gentle spring rain falls softly on the windshield. A farmer with a hoe unhurriedly walks along the tree-lined country road enjoying the long-awaited rain.

The rainy country scene has long been a favorite subject of poets and painters. When the misty air hangs low over the mountains, small clusters of houses surrounded by fresh green fields are possessed by an eternal beauty.

On rainy days when the crops are in, farmers gather at the village wine shop to share stories and enjoy a leisurely cup of rice wine.

First I draw the water into the paddy field,
then I weed the cotton well to make it yield.
Pluck cucumbers underneath the hedge
and pound the barley with a small stone wedge.
When wine is mellow at the neighbors',
we shall set in the arbor and rest from our labors.

—Yi Jung Bo (18th century)

THE MIRACLE WORKERS

Korea's phoenixlike rise from the ashes of the Korean War to a booming industrial nation is a true economic miracle. The leadership of President Park Chung Hee, the foresight of Korea's economic planners, and the determined efforts and national pride of Korea's labor force have moved the Hermit Kingdom into the age of modern technology and made it a strong competitor in all the world markets.

Japan must be credited with laying the foundation for the development of industry in Korea between 1910 and 1945. The colonial government built roads and railroads, electric power stations, communication networks. It established mines and factories, and modernized the monetary and banking systems. This was for Japan's benefit, of course. Most of the consumer goods produced in small-scale factories and cottage industries were for export to Japan. Japan brought its own skilled laborers and administrators to Korea and discouraged Koreans from obtaining positions of responsibility or management. That the common Korean laborer was looked down on was nothing new. He had always worked for someone else—the ruler or a landlord—so there was little to motivate or reward him. When liberation finally came, the new Korean managers—lacking experience and self-confidence—had to struggle along as best they could. Chaos and corruption were widespread.

The dawning of a new era. Since the 1960s the nation has switched its emphasis from agriculture to industrialization. Employees of the Pohang Iron and Steel Company on the southeastern coast bicycle off to begin the 6:00 A.M. shift. The expansion of new industry has drawn many young people away from their villages and created a new working class.

The Korean War dealt a severe blow. When the peninsula was divided at the 38th Parallel, most of Korea's heavy industry and power-generating facilities ended up in the North, and what industries there were in the South were either in ruins or were operating below capacity, even though the demand for goods was high. The housing shortage was acute because of the widespread destruction. Natural resources were few: South Korea had coal but not iron ore or oil; the soil was poor and arable land was scarce; forests had been depleted by careless overuse. Chaos and corruption persisted. As far as anyone could tell, Korea was a hopeless case.

Through the 1950s almost all consumer goods and machinery were imported, and the prevailing attitude was that anything made in a foreign country must be better than the domestic product. Cynical jokes were common. A shopper might inquire, "Is this a good pencil?" "Of course it is," would reply the shopkeeper, "It wasn't made in Korea."

The turnabout came when Army General Park Chung Hee established a new government in 1961. Almost immediately, General Park set new national priorities and drew up plans for controlled economic growth. The previous government under Syngman Rhee had felt that the reunification of the peninsula must precede industrial development. But the realization that negotiation with the North on equal terms required economic strength led to the establishment of clear economic goals. Thus national industrial development and political aspirations were linked, and public and private enterprises all began working toward the same end.

Economic assistance from the United States after World War II, and again after the Korean War, helped shape the pattern of development. To reach the ultimate goal of export-oriented industrialization and self-reliance, a series of five-year plans was developed with the aid of foreign experts and international advisers. The First Five-Year Plan (1962–66) concentrated on the development of electric power and fuel sources as a basis for the expansion of industry, self-sufficiency in grain production, and the building of roads and dams and other public works.

Most of the goals of the First Five-Year Plan were not only met but surpassed. The Second and Third plans that followed had similar success. Shipbuilding, steel, petrochemical, and electronic industries expanded; the dependence on foreign savings was nearly eliminated; rural and household incomes became competitive. Everywhere the standard of living and quality of life improved. Per capita income was $95 in 1961; in 1978 it was over $1,000.

Many factors were responsible for this phenomenal growth. Since 1961, the capital required for industrial development has come through international loans and investments by foreign countries, primarily the United States and Japan. This foreign capital brought with it modern technology, management know-how, and marketing experience. The authority of the government has also made a big difference. Having shrewdly assessed the availability of foreign markets, it was able to develop a strategy aimed at them and then to secure the cooperation of industry. Long-term planning continues today, and while the highly centralized government exercises considerable influence on the business sector, business in turn enjoys government support and subsidies that help minimize risks.

Yet all of these factors depended on the Korean labor force in order to be effective. Thousands upon thousands of young workers flocked from the countryside to the major cities to take part in the economic boom. Accepting relatively low wages, they were young, educated, disciplined, and hardworking. It is this generation that has truly earned the title "the miracle workers."

Also participating in the economic boom is a new breed of young industrialists. Kim Byung-mahn, a law school graduate in his mid-thirties, has in just four years turned a small plastics shop into a hundred-million-dollar business with more than five thousand employees and regional offices in nine foreign countries. He is only one of many with similar success stories achieved by constant hard work. Taking but little time for recreation and abhoring the cocktail-and-golf-course method of doing business, Kim can be found wearing baggy casual clothes and dusty shoes, constantly supervising his factories and mingling with his employees.

The ever-growing industries, professional fields, and new agricultural technology have had a dramatic effect on employment. Before 1960 college graduates were not always able to find jobs in their professions, leaving them to while away their time in tea rooms and pool halls or to work as mailmen or common laborers. Today job recruiters seek out potential employees before graduation, and students can look forward to very good salaries. Although the size of the labor force has grown, a result of the increased population as well as the large numbers of young women entering the job market, the number of jobs available has grown even faster. Overall employment in 1976 was 96 percent, creating acute shortages in some fields.

Seoul and Pusan were the first large industrial centers because as major cities they had resources, people, and available transportation, including facilities for shipping. As industries boomed, they concentrated in these two areas, contributing to the housing shortage, crowded urban conditions, and pollution. In an effort to alleviate these conditions, new industrial complexes are being developed throughout Korea in rural areas and previously undeveloped coastal towns. These industrial complexes include technological training schools, housing, and educational and medical facilities for their employees. Posters and slogans abound, and in the national spirit of hard work and competition they exhort workers to do their best and maintain high standards. Team activities and physical fitness are encouraged, and it is common for a factory's entire personnel to turn out for exercises on their lunch hour. Some company employees will stay after work is over for a class in flower arranging or pottery.

Heavy industry has been so successful that, in addition to meeting domestic needs, exports are increasing tremendously. The Pohang Iron and Steel Company was a landmark development when it was dedicated in 1973. In contrast to the past when almost all industrial iron and steel were imported, more than $401 million worth of Korean iron and steel was exported in 1976. South Korea's only cement factory was destroyed in the Korean War, but the country is now the fifth largest exporter of cement. Ships, cars, trucks, machinery, construction, textiles, electronics—the list could go on and on, each with its own success story.

Korea also exports its best resource—its labor force. Korean construction firms are busy all over the world building highways, apartment buildings, and harbors in the Mideast, Southeast Asia, Africa, and Latin America. Most of the construction contracts are awarded by countries in the Middle East, and the Korean construction industry is currently shifting its emphasis from domestic to overseas activities.

Although industry and construction are dramatic examples of the growth and development enjoyed in the last two decades, nearly every aspect of Korean life has been touched by the advance into the modern age of technology. Life expectancy, a healthy 68 years in 1976, is expected to reach 72.7 years by 1981, and a middle-school education will soon become compulsory. Advances in farming, housing, communications, and transportation are all part of the new Korea. But there is one group of people whose contribution to the new society cannot be ignored. Abandoning their overprotected and restricted role dictated by the Confucian ethics of the Yi dynasty, Korea's women are emerging as a dynamic part of the labor force and as productive, contributing members of a vibrant society.

Economic planners have steered the country from its reliance on first agriculture and then textiles and other light industries into the more sophisticated field of heavy industries. This was a great achievement. But no matter how disciplined and diligent the Korean labor force, the prospect for development in the long term depends increasingly on the international political and economic climate.

Dressed like medieval warriors to protect themselves from the intense heat of the molten iron, these men strain to meet the ever-growing demand for iron and steel by the heavy-industry and construction boom. Using iron ore from the United States and Australia, the Pohang Iron and Steel Company is the nation's first integrated iron and steel mill. Completed in 1973, it has a capacity of over a million tons of crude steel a year. The company provides dormitories, schools, and medical facilities for its employees, and it has changed the small coastal town of Pohang into a busy industrial complex bustling with young steelworkers.

Producing everything from supertankers to the sporty passenger car "Pony," Hyundai Industries has become one of the largest manufacturers in the world. The diligence of the Korean worker has earned recognition in the international marketplace.

Surrounded by the evidence of modern technology, these auto workers enjoy playing *changgi*, an ancient Korean game of chess, on their lunch break.

Welders are in great demand. Many companies set up their own technical schools to train new industrial workers, and a profession once looked down upon finds a new place and a new purpose in society.

Factory slogans exhort industriousness and quality control. A young woman in a cosmetics factory wears a slogan saying "Prevent Inferior Products" attached to her name tag as a constant reminder.

The faces of the new generation. Women are slowly relocating their sense of security; while it was once firmly lodged in marriage, now it rests increasingly outside the home, in jobs, or at least job potential. "I encourage my students to become productive, contributing members of society." Dr. Kim Okgill, former Minister of Education and president of Ewha Women's University, has devoted her life to improving the role of women in society. Established by Protestant missionaries in 1886, Ewha is now one of the largest women's universities in the world. Much loved by her students, Dr. Kim often invites them to her home to share *nang-myun*, her "famous" dish of buckwheat noodles in cold soup.

Autumn is most beautiful at Maple Rock—
My best songs ring across your vales.
Soft, the early falling frost

embroiders the ten thousand hills and dales.
Alone I sit on a hanging rock
and forget the world and home.

BUDDHISM AND OTHER BELIEFS

Korea is a land of many religions that blend and merge in daily life. One may follow the compassionate path of the Buddha while one's relationships with others are guided by Confucian ethics. And both of these religions find themselves compatible with the Taoist objective of happiness and long life and with the Shamanistic worship of the gods of nature. The search for harmony is surely greater than any single religion, and truth can be sought in a combination of beliefs.

The oldest religion in Korea is based on the primitive Koreans' first attempts to understand and come to terms with their environment. These early people believed that the objects and forces of nature were controlled by powerful spirits, and they held ceremonies honoring and seeking the good will of the local gods and the supreme god, Hananim, at planting and harvest times. Families carried out annual rites for the spirits of their ancestors; villages conducted rites to the mountain god, the god of the village shrine, and the Dragon God of the Sea; clans and kingdoms established shrines in honor of their founders.

Shamans had an important role in society. Able to contact the spirits, they conducted rites for the spirit gods in the village ceremonies and attempted to cure illness by driving the evil spirits out of the body. In Korea the shamans were usually women, and they are still found in rural areas. The village ceremonies are now rarely conducted, for their meaning has been dimmed by time; but the shrines to the village god and the mountain god still stand.

A lone figure kneeling in the great hall of a Buddhist temple bows before the altar. The bell and wooden clapper are used by the priests to accompany their chanting. Buddhists believe that the Eternal Buddha always appears before people in the most friendly forms and shows to them the wisest methods of relief.

During the Three Kingdoms period, from about the first to the seventh century, other religions began to reach Korea by way of China. The first of these was Taoism. The source of harmony, the origin of the order in the world, between heaven and earth, *yin* and *yang*, is the Tao. Tao means literally "a way" or by extension "the way of nature." And according to the philosopher Lao Tzu, the aim of human existence is to attain harmony with the Tao and thus find peace and enlightenment. This can only be done by letting things take their natural course. Taoism was compatible with the indigenous nature worship in Korea and through the years it freely borrowed the gods and ceremonies of Buddhism and Confucianism. Taoism did not flourish as an independent religion in Korea, but it has left its mark through its emphasis on the search for happiness and longevity, patience, simplicity, contentment, and harmony.

In the sixth century B.C., Buddhism was founded in India by Gautama Buddha, who was looking for a new, moderate philosophy of living that would enable people to find salvation and reach *nirvana*. In the Four Noble Truths, the Buddha set forth his idea that suffering is universal and caused by selfish desire, and that the way to remove desire and thereby relieve suffering is to follow the Noble Eightfold Path and its rules for a virtuous life. Thus Buddhism was originally a godless religion, centered instead on a system of philosophical principles for avoiding earthly suffering and an endless cycle of reincarnation.

As Buddhism spread it evolved into two great

schools of doctrine, and of these it is Mahayana, or "Greater Vehicle," Buddhism that eventually reached Korea. This form of Buddhism offers salvation by faith and by good works for oneself and others. Though differences over methods have led to the formation of numerous sects, Mahayana, as its name suggests, is broad and inclusive in its outlook. On its way to Korea through China, it absorbed a variety of superstitions and beliefs and acquired an elaborate hierarchy of deities, saints, and guardians. It also adopted local rituals where it became established. Almost every Buddhist temple in Korea has a shrine to the local mountain god; usually portrayed as an old man with a tiger, the mountain god is duly venerated lest the spirits on whose land the temple stands become angry!

Buddhism reached the Three Kingdoms in the fourth century A.D. By the sixth century Buddhism was so firmly established that priests, scriptures, and artifacts were being sent on to Japan. Eventually Buddhism was adopted as the state religion in the Three Kingdoms. Royal patronage during the Golden Age of Unified Silla and the enthusiastic support of the Koryo dynasty caused a great flowering of temples and art. During the fourteenth century every third son of a Korean family was expected to become a Buddhist priest, and there were more than eighty thousand temples. Gradually priests became politicians and members of the court, where they gained power; many became corrupt. During the Yi dynasty the influence of Buddhism was removed from the government, and Confucianism was recognized as the state religion.

Dating from the sixth century B.C., Confucianism was originally less a religion than a system of ethics for harmonizing all the relationships within the family and the state, As centuries passed, Confucius and his disciples were deified by their followers, and temples and shrines were built and rites and ceremonies conducted in their honor. Many writings and commentaries, the most famous of which are the *Analects* collected by his disciples, set forth Confucius's teachings.

The essence of these teachings lies in Confucius's formulation of the "Five Great Relationships" fundamental to social order: between ruler and subject; father and son; husband and wife; older brother and younger brother; and older friend and younger friend. Later, Confucius's disciples evolved the Ten Attitudes by which the Five Great Relationships should be governed: love in the father and filial piety in the son; gentility in the eldest brother and humility and respect in the younger; righteous behavior in the husband and obedience in the wife; humane consideration in elders and deference in juniors; and benevolence in rulers and loyalty in subjects.

The Confucian classics probably came to Korea with the earliest written material from China, and all of the Three Kingdoms have left evidence of early Confucian influence. Confucianism was embraced so eagerly that the Chinese referred to Korea as "the Land of Eastern Decorum," and there was a Confucian university in Koguryo in the fourth century A.D.

Confucianism in Korea meant a system of education, ceremony, and civil administration. The institutionalization of Confucian principles of government resulted in a system of civil-service examinations. The examinations were based entirely on the Confucian classics and commentaries, calligraphy, and the writing of poetry and essays. Theoretically this should have resulted in a government based on merit, but in practice wealth and influence could buy positions.

In the seventeenth century, as news of the outside world began to enter Korea, a new philosophical school arose. Called Sirhak, or "Practical Learning," it repudiated orthodox Confucian teachings and urged a scientific, reasoned approach to agriculture, defense, and trade. The world was changing, but Confucianism failed to respond. It stagnated through the years of invasions and turmoil, and with the Japanese occupation in 1910 it was discarded as a basis for government and administration. But the Confucian heritage in Korea is clearly seen in the country's social stability, in the customs governing family relationships, and in the people's reverence for age and respect for learning.

The first Catholic writings also reached Korea in the seventeenth century from the Chinese court in Peking, but the first priest did not arrive until 1785, when the Jesuit Fr. Peter Grammont crossed the border secretly. Foreign religions were banned, and converts and priests were persecuted over the next century until 1876, when treaties were signed with Western nations ensuring the safety and freedom of Christian missionaries. The first Protestant missionary to arrive was Dr. Horace N. Allen in 1884. The Presbyterians and Methodists were the most successful in gaining converts and have the largest membership among Protestant churches in Korea today.

Christianity had a great impact on the Korea of the nineteenth and twentieth centuries. Missionaries brought the modern knowledge that Korea needed in every field, as well as the Western concepts of democracy and individualism. Church schools, by promoting the native *han'gul* alphabet, increased the rate of literacy, and by emphasizing the importance of the individual they improved the status of women. Missionaries also helped many of Korea's young potential leaders obtain higher educations abroad and gave direct support to the resistance to Japan and the independence movement. Although there are more than twice as many Buddhists as Christians, Christianity has provided a source of leadership and new ideals for the emerging modern Korea.

In addition to the major religions of Buddhism, Confucianism, Christianity, and the indigenous Shamanism, there are many modern religious sects that originated in the Tonghak Movement in the 1860s. *Tonghak* means "Eastern Learning" as opposed to "Western Learning" or Catholicism. Founded by Choe Che-u, a country scholar and minor aristocrat, it was basically a rural reform movement opposing political decadence and the oppression of people in rural areas. The theology combined Confucianism, Buddhism, and Taoism in a belief of a better future. The government eventually put down the Tonghak armies and executed Choe, but the movement survived, changing its emphasis from politics to religious nationalism, and its name to Chondogyo. The Tonghak Movement is the basis of numerous smaller sects, some of which are ultranationalistic, and all of which combine Confucian ethics, Buddhist rites, and Taoist religious practices. Such a mixture reflects the diversity of faiths found in Korean society.

大雄寶殿
虛空境界豈思量
不離祇園大道場

Drums and chanting echo in the darkness of 3:00 A.M., announcing the beginning of a new day. At 7:00 the novices march to the great hall for prayers.

Nestled in remote mountains and surrounded by ancient pine trees and clear streams, Woonmun-sa temple is one of the few for women who wish to become Buddhist priests. Each young woman must be sponsored by a priest and spend six years at the convent in preparation. When she enters she shaves her head and takes a religious name such as Sae Dung, which means "Enlightenment of Mankind."

The steady hand of the head priest demonstrates the art of calligraphy to a group of students. Since the Buddhist scriptures are written in Chinese, the students must spend many hours mastering the complicated Chinese characters. Like on a college campus, the daily schedules of the students take them from building to building.

A game of volleyball brings laughter to the novices. Twice a day between classes and chores, free time is spent for entertainment or relaxation. Badminton, pingpong, and volleyball are popular games.

Many novices also enjoy quiet walks around the temple grounds. The pavilion in the background houses the great drum and bell that can be heard for miles on a still morning.

One of four militant kings who defend the heavenly realm, this fierce guardian stands at the temple entrance to ward off evil spirits and protect the truth of the Buddha. Visitors to Chikchi-sa temple burn incense before the golden image of the Buddha that is surrounded by a thousand smaller Buddhas. No two of the thousand Buddhas have the same expression, for each is an individualized image of an eternal spiritual concept.

How can there be a likeness
to your virtues,
untouched by foe or obstacle,
Everlasting, unlimited, and
which cannot be surpassed?

—Hymn to the Buddha
of Infinite Compassion,
Satapancasatka of Matrceta

The eighth day of the fourth lunar month marks the Buddha's birthday. Tens of thousands of followers gather at temples throughout the land to celebrate his coming. Seas of lanterns are hung in the temple yards. Streamers proclaim the names of the faithful with words of peace and blessings for long life.

A woman pours a libation of water over an image of the young Buddha.

On the morning of Chusok, Korean Thanksgiving Day, the eldest male member of the family conducts a ceremony in memory of the ancestors. Food and fruits of the recent harvest are prepared as an offering to the last several generations. These rites have had an important role in the structure of family life since prehistoric times, but the rituals have been shaped and refined by Confucianism.

A family visits a gravesite to pay their proper respects on occasions such as holidays, anniversaries of deaths, and birthdays. These rituals strengthen the family ties that are the foundation of Korean society.

A humble believer hopefully watches the burning rice paper as the *mudang* tosses it into the air. The *mudang* is a shaman or sorceress who can intercede with the spirits for those seeking good luck or a blessing. Money is offered before the altar, and the *mudang* chants the person's name and wishes in order to contact the proper spirit. This is a form of spirit worship dating from prehistoric times, and shamans are still hired to exorcise evil spirits or seek success for a struggling business. It is not surprising that Shamanism is still found in modern society since Korean life and philosophy are based on a feeling of closeness to nature and a belief in the presence of spirits within.

BY THE SEA

Almost completely surrounded by water, Korea has survived the constant threat of invasion from the sea, developed one of the world's largest seaports, and found a major source of protein in the sea's harvest. Small fishing villages dot the spectacularly beautiful coastline with its rugged rock formations, white sandy beaches, lagoons, and tidal flats.

Small farms nestle in the steep narrow valleys of the foothills of the T'aebaek Mountains that closely parallel the eastern coast. The tidal ranges of the Sea of Japan (called the East Sea in Korea) are relatively small, and the water is deep immediately offshore. Tourists are especially attracted to the scenery of the east coast, with its white sandy beaches, clear water, and pine trees.

In contrast, the west coast is made up of alluvial plains and muddy tidal flats. The murky water of the shallow Yellow Sea, with its tidal range of up to thirty feet—second greatest in the world—exposes vast silted muddy flats, shoals, and low-lying islands at low tide. Along the coast are many small ports and hundreds of tiny islands, and there is extensive farming on the fertile plains of the Han and Kum rivers and on land that has been reclaimed by diking shallow arms of the sea.

The south coast is full of small bays, peninsulas, and islands formed when hills in ages past were drowned. The tides and mud flats are not as great as on the west coast, nor are there sea cliffs since the many islands protect the mainland. But the narrow channels between the islands are known for their extremely fast currents.

Weh Dol Guay, a lonesome rock off the coast of Sogwipo on the southern part of Cheju Island, typifies the natural beauty of the rock formations found in many coastal areas of the peninsula. Such unusual rock formations carved by centuries of wind and water offer extraordinary beauty that attracts tourists and honeymooners from the mainland.

Fishing is excellent due to the shallow continental shelfs of the Yellow Sea and East China Sea (or South Sea) and the seasonal interchange of warm and cold currents in the Sea of Japan. But until recently fishing was only done by people living near the sea to supplement their agriculture. With 10,950 miles of coastline and abundant resources including more than seventy-five species of fish, the fishing industry had great potential. Since 1960, both coastal fishing and deep-sea fishing have been developed with new techniques and refrigeration, and Korea now has the world's seventh-largest fishing industry and ranks fourth in fishery exports. With conservation, pollution controls, fish breeding, and new equipment, the industry can expect to reach new heights.

More than three thousand islands dot the rugged coastline, mostly around the west side and southern tip of the peninsula. Few of them are very large, but many are known for the beauty of their rock formations. Ullung Island in the Sea of Japan is famous for its cuttlefish that are hung up on racks and dried in the sun. Kanghwa Island near Seoul has served as the temporary home of exiled kings throughout Korea's history. Hansan Island among the southern coastal islands was the scene of Admiral Yi's battles with his famous ironclad "turtle ships." And Cheju Island further off the southern coast is a tropical paradise.

Kanghwa Island has had an important role in the nation's history ever since the legendary founder, Tan'gun, established an altar in 2333 B.C. on the summit of Mt. Mani, the island's highest peak. Remnants can still be seen of numerous fortresses that were built on the mainland side of the island to protect exiled kings in the mid-thirteenth century. Prehistoric dolmens, twelfth-century celadon pottery, ginseng, and temples are all part of Kanghwa's fame.

As is known to all students of naval history, Admiral Yi Sun-shin's "turtle ships," whose plated decks made them the world's first ironclads, were remarkably effective in protecting Korea from the threat of Japanese invasion in the sixteenth century. The Japanese military leader, Hideyoshi, was trying to conquer the Chinese Ming empire, and desired free passage through Korea. But when this was refused he attacked. Admiral Yi established his base of operations on Hansan Island and, battling among the many islands of the south coast, defeated the invading Japanese ships. A statue of Admiral Yi in full armor and holding his sword in both hands stands at a memorial shrine in Tongyong. Inscribed on his sword is a poem he wrote:

I pledge to the sea—
The fish and dragons are
moved to take my part;
I swear by the hill—
The plants and the trees know
my heart.

Called the "Hawaii of the Orient," tropical Cheju Island has become a popular tourist resort. Its southern climate and distance of sixty miles from the mainland have helped it develop and retain customs that are quite different from those in the rest of Korea. Mt. Halla, which rises in the center of the island, is a volcanic cone that has not been active since A.D. 1007. Standing 6,450 feet high, it is the highest peak in all of South Korea and is surrounded by 360 smaller extinct volcanoes. The area's various lava formations, tunnels, pillars, caves, and waterfalls attract much interest. Meadows gently sloping toward the sea are covered with bright yellow coleseed flowers in the spring.

Dragon's Pool, the Grotto of the Serpent, and Heaven Lake Falls are just a few of the scenic spots where legend and nature combine in incredible beauty. The Cave of the Three Family Spirits on the northern slope of Mt. Halla near Cheju City is surrounded by gnarled old pine trees. Legend says that from this cave appeared three gods named Ko and Bu and Yang. One day they found a wooden box drifting ashore, and when they opened the box three beautiful women stepped out, all elegantly dressed in blue. They carried with them the seeds of five grains, a cow, an ox, horses, and many servants. The god-men married the three beautiful women and thus established the families of Ko, Bu, and Yang. The majority of the people living on Cheju today belong to these three families and still hold memorial services at the cave twice a year, in spring and fall.

Because of the sea winds and tropical storms, Cheju houses are built low, are surrounded by rock walls, and have their traditional thatched roofs tied down with rope nets. Even orchards are protected by rock walls to block the Cheju winds. Cheju Island is less densely populated than the peninsula and is a potential site for the development of new villages and farms. New housing uses modern materials, and tile roofs are replacing the less practical thatched roofs of the past.

Large ranches have provided breeding stock for centuries, and over 60 percent of Korea's horses are on the island. Sogwipo on the southern side is the citrus center of Korea. Oranges, grapefruits, tangerines, and pineapples thrive in the tropical climate. Cheju oranges were traditionally used as tribute payment to the royal courts. Now yearly citrus proceeds exceed eight million dollars.

The women divers of Cheju are legendary in their ability to withstand the coldest water. Wearing one-piece white cotton suits, they can stay submerged from three to four minutes at depths of forty to sixty feet collecting abalone and seaweed. They learn to swim and dive at an early age, and all year round women divers from ages sixteen to sixty can be found waiting for the tides or plying their trade. One wonders if any of them have glimpsed the legendary treasures of the Dragon King of the Sea:

Once long ago the best-loved daughter of the Dragon King of the Sea fell ill and no one was able to cure her. Then the tortoise came forward and said, "Exalted King, I have heard that the best cure is the liver of a young rabbit and I think I know where to find one."

So the Dragon King sent the tortoise off to the seashore to bring back the rabbit. When he at last reached the shore the tortoise soon met a curious rabbit, who greeted him politely.

"I have come to admire the view of the sea from these green hills," said the tortoise.

"And does it please you, honored sir?" asked the rabbit.

"It is very dull," said the tortoise. "It cannot compare with the beauties and treasures of the sea—the waving jade green plants, the hills of coral, and the processions of fish the colors of the rainbow. You should see these wonders for yourself."

"Oh, I should like to," said the rabbit, "but I cannot swim."

"You could travel there on my back," answered the tortoise. "I will go very slowly and carefully and teach you how to breathe under water."

Thus the rabbit learned to breathe under water and enjoyed all the sights and wonders that the tortoise had promised. But one day he overheard one of the palace guards say to another, "Today the Dragon King's daughter will surely recover when she eats the liver of the rabbit."

The rabbit was dismayed but he showed no fear when they came for him. He bowed politely to the Dragon King and said, "Why did the tortoise not tell me it was my liver that you wanted? Didn't he know that when the Heavenly King made us rabbits, he gave us the power to take our livers out of our bodies? I had just washed my liver and put it out in the sun to dry when I met the tortoise and now we will have to go back and get it."

The Dragon King and the tortoise believed him and the tortoise let the rabbit climb on his back and swam across the ocean to the sandy beach.

"Where is your liver, honorable rabbit?" asked the tortoise.

"Ai, it's safe inside my body!" laughed the rabbit. And away he hopped as fast as he could.

***Following page*: Banners on long bamboo poles and music blaring through loudspeakers on the boats celebrate the happy return of the fishermen, their boats low in the water with the heavy load of the day's catch.**

Warmed by the evening sun, the farmer washes his feet in a stream at the end of a long day of harvesting wheat. The young rice seedlings are waiting to be transplanted to the empty terraced paddies. As in many coastal villages, the people in this village engage in both farming and fishing.

CHEJU ISLAND

The southernmost island of Korea, Cheju is known for its strong winds, many rocks, and numerous women. This volcanic island of caves, waterfalls, and rock formations preserves many of its traditional customs. The highest mountain in South Korea is here, Mt. Halla, soaring 6,450 feet above sea level and surrounded by tropical plants and flowers that are found only on Cheju.

Woman divers gather abalone and seaweed, and citrus fruits grow in the tropical climate. Sweet potatoes in the fall and garlic in the spring are harvested from the rocky soil, and "grandfather stones" carved of lava rock guard the village gates. In the 1980s Cheju Island will be developed as an international harbor and tourist's paradise.

The children of Cheju amuse themselves swimming and fishing in the clear streams. The water is clear and young boys quickly learn to spear fish with a sharp stick. It is a treat to go out with a group of friends, spearing fish and eating them raw with a drink of wine. The island is also known as an ideal spot for sport fishing and pheasant hunting.

Surrounded by lava-rock walls, their thatched roofs tied down with rope nets, these low houses are protected from the high winds that sweep in from the sea. Such homes are disappearing fast and being replaced by modern buildings. The government is

trying to preserve this unique Cheju Island architecture by offering funds to homeowners in the hope they will be persuaded to repair and not demolish their old homes. Even with modernization, Cheju will retain its distinctive charm.

Pigs and chickens change hands every fifth day as farmers bring their goods to the village market. In a mood of festivity women are tempted by the wares of the basket maker, the brass merchant, and the yardgoods seller. Children run about getting underfoot and the men sometimes enjoy a drink of wine with friends. Vendors set up temporary stalls under cloth awnings or spread out their wares on mats laid over the dusty ground.

At the end of ten years' work
I have a hut with a straw roof.
The clear wind lives in one half,

and the bright moon in the other.
There's no space to invite the hills—
they will have to stay outside.

—Song Sun (1493–1583)

LIFE'S CELEBRATIONS

Music, singing, and dancing have been a part of everyday Korean life since prehistoric times. Farmers' bands play as the laborers move from field to field, and any occasion is an excuse to sing. Life's celebrations—births, birthdays, weddings, and funerals—bring out special holiday clothes, lots of food and wine, and the revival of old traditions, although today they may not be as elaborate as they once were.

Holiday clothes are especially bright and gay for young women and children, who may appear in all the colors of the rainbow. Their elders prefer more sedate soft grays and blues. Women wear the long flowing skirts and short blouses of embroidered silk that came into use during the fifteenth century, and men and boys wear a vest or jacket with loose trousers tied at the ankles.

The birth of a child, especially the birth of the first son who will carry on the ancestral rites, is naturally an exciting event. In earlier times, if a child lived for one hundred days it had survived the most dangerous period of its life, and a small feast was given in celebration. Family, relatives, and neighbors still gather on this occasion to eat rice cakes and red bean cakes, which are also sent to all the villagers in hopes of long life for the child. Gifts are received in return, such as a skein of thread for long life or money or rice symbolizing wealth.

Red peppers and pieces of charcoal hung high across the gatepost announce the birth of a son. The *inchul* rope protects the newborn from evil spirits and bars visitors from the home for several weeks. The custom is a reminder of the time in the past when infants—very susceptible to disease—suffered a high mortality rate.

The first birthday calls for an even larger party: more rice cakes are sent out, gifts are received, and the child toddles about to everyone's amusement dressed in the Yi-dynasty costume of an unmarried youth, with its black hood, colorful jacket, and baggy pants. The birthday table is decorated with an assortment of cakes, fruits, thread, writing brushes, books, money, and rice. If the child selects money or rice he may gain great wealth; cake or food means a destiny as a government official; and a bow might indicate a great warrior!

A person reaching sixty years of age was rare until modern times and was considered to have lived a long life indeed. Today the sixtieth birthday is still an occasion for honor and celebration; the party held may be the family's biggest event ever. The sons and grandsons first send out a great many invitations. Often a restaurant or hall is rented if the home is not large enough to accommodate all of the guests. In fact, there may be so many people attending that, in rural villages, straw mats and canopies will be set up outside and the party will go on for several days.

The old couple, dressed as though they were newly married, sit at the main table with piles of cakes and fruits in front of them. Sons and daughters bow and offer wine to their parents, and then grandchildren, cousins, and friends offer their respects. There is much singing and dancing while the family members behave like children and try to make their parents feel young again.

Other birthdays are not forgotten but are celebrated on a smaller scale unless there is a special occasion to mark such as graduation or a new job. And of course to reach the age of seventy is cause for a repetition of the sixtieth birthday party!

Marriage had special importance in the days when the bride joined her husband's family and everyone had a say in the matter, not just the bride and groom. Today, young people are more likely to meet and fall in love, marry, and form their own household. But the traditions governing the preliminaries, the engagement ceremony, and the wedding are still strong. The families of the two young people first examine the couple's "Four Pillars"—the year, month, day, and hour of birth—for these will help determine their fortune. Then a fortune teller is consulted to discover the chances of marital harmony. If the signs are auspicious, the next step is the engagement ceremony. At this time the families meet and exchange gifts and plan the date of the wedding ceremony.

On the eve of the wedding, the groom's family usually sends a servant or friends of the groom to the bride's house with a large box. They arrive at night shouting, "Buy a box!" and do not give it up until treated to a small feast or gift of money. In the box will be a gift of jewelry or the red and blue fabric for the wedding dress.

The traditional wedding takes place in the bride's home, and sometimes it is necessary to set up a large canopy in the courtyard. The couple, wearing Yi-dynasty costumes, stand on opposite sides of a high table and exchange bows and sips of wine. On the table are wooden mandarin ducks symbolizing conjugal fidelity, red and blue threads for long life, and candles.

On their wedding night the newlyweds are subject to much teasing and giggling. The bride's brothers and sisters moisten their fingers in order to poke little holes in the rice-paper doors of the couple's room so they can peep in. Only after the bridegroom has removed the bride's headdress, untied her coat string, and removed one of her socks may he extinguish the candle to gain a little privacy.

Today many young couples are likely to be married at a wedding hall in a Western-style ceremony complete with flowers and bridesmaids, and to leave afterward on a honeymoon trip. But still they must pay their proper respects to their parents and expect much teasing and hilarity at a large reception after the wedding.

There are many customs and superstitions associated with old-style Korean funerals. In this as in other celebrations during a person's life, the family joins together to demonstrate their honor, respect, and filial piety. When death is imminent, the family gathers. The house is cleaned, and the patient is dressed in clean clothes and put in a clean room, his head toward the east. If it is the master of the house that is dying, only the men are allowed to stay in the room to observe the last breath; similarly, only women will attend a dying mistress. When it is seen that death has come, the body is covered with a quilt and loud grief-stricken wailing commences.

Hoping that the dead may yet return to life, one of the male relatives may climb up onto the roof to wave the dead person's coat and call three times for the soul to return. When it does not, the finality of death must be accepted. The family then goes into mourning by wearing simple white clothes and begins preparations for the funeral. They must send out obituary notices, prepare sacrificial food, build the coffin, and begin sewing hempen funeral clothes. The corpse is bathed and dressed in new clothes and a red funeral banner is prepared.

From the day of death until the burial, meals of the deceased's favorite fcods are placed before his casket. The funeral may take place on the third or fifth day after death. A longer delay is considered ostentatious, although in the old days a prominent family might have delayed up to the fortieth day and royalty even longer.

The red funeral banner and lanterns lead the colorfully decorated bier in the funeral procession. A bell ringer helps keep the singing in unison and the family, friends, and villagers follow behind. In large funerals a second bier with a false coffin is sometimes included to deceive the evil spirits, and devil chasers with grotesque masks and burning faggots trail along the roadsides to prevent the evil spirits from coming near.

At the cemetery a geomancer selects the gravesite by calculating the most auspicious spot. The Korean word for geomancy, which translates as "wind and water," reflects a long-established respect for the relationship of nature to life. A good, natural environment is important for a quiet and happy life on earth, and the earth's energy can be of benefit to man. The vital spots where the earth's energy pours forth can be located by following geomantic doctrine. Such propitious sites are called *myongdang* and are desired for houses, villages, cities, graves, and so on. Today modern cemeteries use this idea in their advertising! Finding a good gravesite is an expression of gratitude and duty to one's ancestors, and by successfully fulfilling their obligations the descendants can expect happiness and prosperity.

These family celebrations, especially weddings, sixtieth birthday parties, and funerals, come at a great expense. Until recently relatives would join together to work, preparing food for feasts that sometimes lasted for days. Affairs are less elaborate now, but naturally it is still difficult for even an ordinary family to afford them; a man's sons may have to save for years in advance, each one putting aside an amount of money every month in a fund especially for the sixtieth birthday celebration or funeral. Marriage involves the exchange of gifts, a dowry of household goods, furniture, linens, and the like, as well as a large party. And so parents might also join a group that saves for weddings. Such mutual-aid groups, or *kye*, provide a form of insurance and are also organized for village events, for cooperative farming work, and sometimes even for vacations. Still, the expense of weddings, funerals, and the like is so excessive that the Korean government encourages simplified family rituals.

In recent years, increasing contact with the outside world has led to swift changes in the thinking, feelings, and behavior of the Korean people, with the result that old customs are being modified. In the postwar era, Koreans were exposed to the influence of Western culture. For years after 1945, Soviet forces occupied the North and American troops the South. The South Koreans welcomed the cultural heritage of their American allies, who came to their aid in a time of great national peril, the Korean War, and who put billions of dollars into helping rebuild the war-shattered nation. Traditionally agrarian, Korea in the early 1960s underwent an industrial revolution modeled on Western lines. Fortunately, despite these social changes, Korean society has kept its equanimity and harmony, and has managed to preserve the essence of its heritage.

Being welcomed home for the first time, this baby can look forward to a special celebration on the hundredth day of its life. Rice cakes will be sent to the neighbors as a way of sharing the happiness of the occasion.

An even larger feast will be held on the first birthday. Friends and relatives will be invited, more rice cakes sent out, and gifts exchanged. The child will be dressed in the traditional costume of an unmarried youth and placed before a table on which are arranged a variety of objects such as books and writing brushes, money, rice, cakes, and fruit. If the child picks up a skein of thread he will live a long life; a brush indicates a destiny as a calligrapher. Thus is the future foretold.

The bride greets her parents-in-law for the first time after the marriage ceremony. As tradition dictates, she is adorned with a sparkling headdress while her groom wears the official uniform of a Yi-dynasty civil servant. This is strictly a family affair. The bride bows to her husband's parents, who are seated before a table bearing fruits, chestnuts, and other delicacies, and gifts and greetings are exchanged.

A sixtieth birthday calls for a great celebration. In the old days it was rare to reach the age of sixty. Today it is not so rare, but the occasion is just as happily celebrated. Sons and daughters, relatives, and friends gather for a great banquet, often in a rented hall, to feast and sing and dance to the music of the traditional drum and flute. The old couple sit before a table piled high with cakes and fruits—the more there are and the higher they are piled, the greater the filial piety of the children! Everyone makes merry and encourages the guests of honor to feel young again.

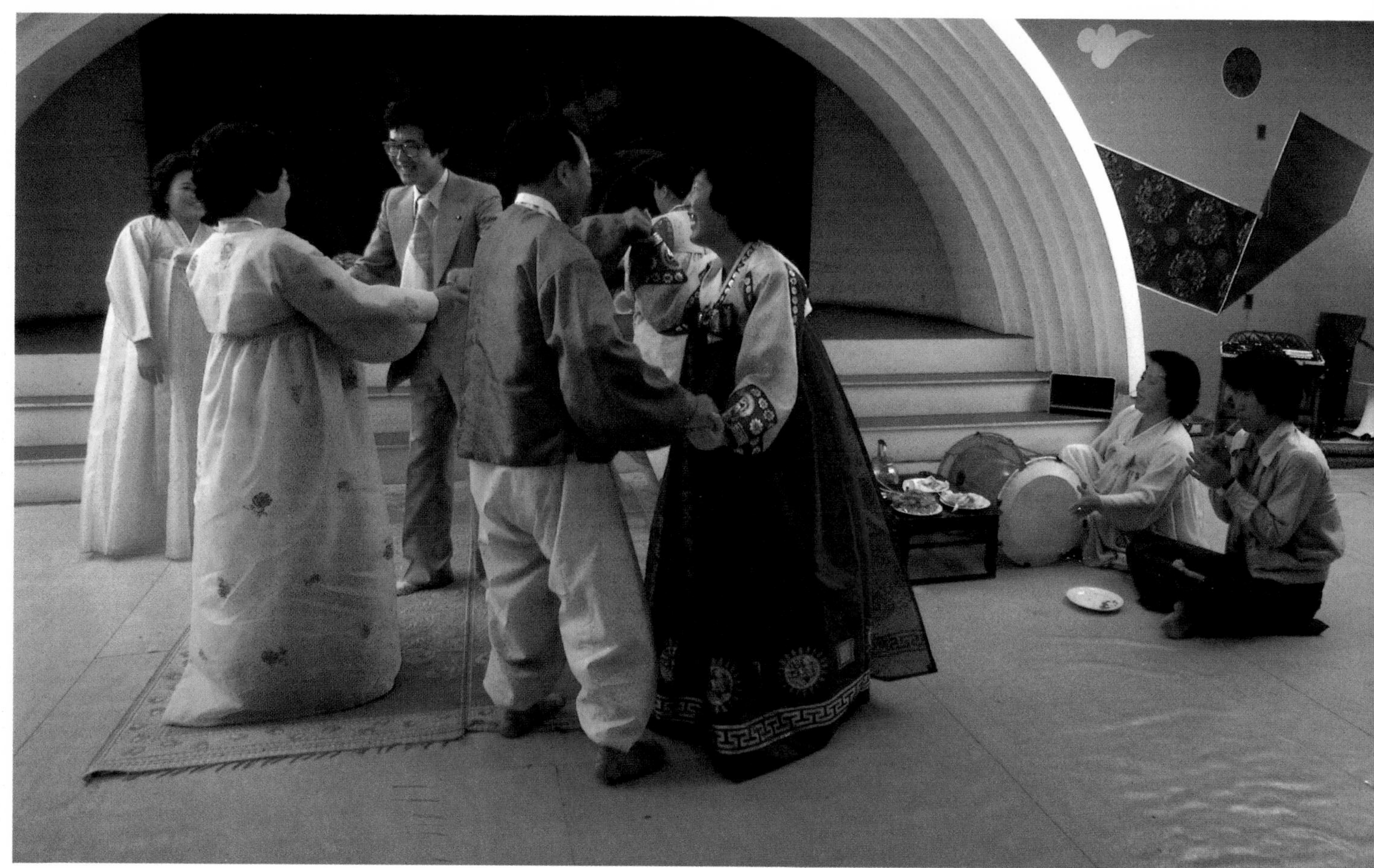

Led by the red banner proclaiming the death of Mr. Chae, the funeral procession passes a harvest rice field near the village of Kwang Yang on the southern tip of the peninsula. Decorated with colorful paper flowers, the bier is carried by villagers in mourning white, while the son and grandson of the deceased follow behind wearing hempen mourning clothes. A bell ringer leads the bier and sings to accompany the lament of the villagers as they proceed to the gravesite.

Now that the burial is over, the son reflects on his relationship with his father and wonders if he could have been a better son.

There is an old Korean folktale about a little family of frogs that conveys the mood of this occasion:

These little frogs always did just the opposite of what their mother told them to do. When the mother was about to die, she called her children to her and said, "When I die, please bury me by the river. Do not bury me on the mountainside," hoping that her children would do just the opposite in their usual way and bury her on the mountain.

When the old mother died the young frogs were so sorry that they had never obeyed their mother. So this time the frogs were determined to do what their mother asked them to do and buried her beside the river.

When it rained the little frogs were afraid the water would rise and wash the grave away, and they would sit on the riverbank and cry with sad, hoarse voices. Today, as they say, frogs still sit and croak whenever it rains.

The long rains have stopped awhile,
the stream begins to clear itself.
Push the boat off, push the boat off!
Shouldering my fishing rod,
I am beside myself with joy.
Chigukch'ong, chigukch'ong, oshwa!
Who could it have been
that made mists, streams, piled peaks?

—Yun Sondo (1587–1671)

THE MAGIC OF GROWING UP

Home is the center of the universe—at least until one is old enough to go to school—and Korean children are loved and indulged, especially by their grandparents. In many homes families of three generations used to live together, so there were many cousins to play with and aunts and uncles and grandparents to tell stories or help make simple toys. Confucian ethics, sometimes seeming very rigid, clearly defined each person's role in the household. Children are still taught to be obedient to their parents and demonstrate proper respect. Boys, and especially the oldest son, must be utterly respectful and obedient to their father, a strict disciplinarian. In turn, the oldest son must be shown respect by his younger brothers and sisters. As children they freely play together and develop strong bonds of affection.

Long ago, boys were given childhood names that would be replaced when they grew up and reached a marriageable age, and girls sometimes were not named at all. But today the name that is given at birth remains the same throughout life. In Korea, a name is said to decide the destiny of its holder, so naturally parents give names of good fortune to their sons and names of beauty or virtue to their daughters. Names that suggest the image of stone or iron, because it is hard and lasts through the ages, are given in the hope of bestowing long life. If a family has lost several children and wishes to avoid the attention of mischievous or evil spirits, the next child may be given a lowly name like "Straw Bag" or "Silly Fool." Altogether, a name will be made up of a clan name, a generation name, and a personal name. And still today it is not unusual for a fortune teller to be consulted in the important task of selecting a suitable name.

Armed with bow and arrow and a cardboard box for a shield, the imagination of a child of seven magically turns him into Ju Mong, the legendary archer of Koguryo. The early Koreans of that period were known for their archery and horsemanship, and their exploits are depicted in mural paintings in the tombs of Koguryo kings.

When a child is old enough to go to school, proud parents send him off with great expectations. Until recently, when an elementary student reached the fourth grade tutors were hired and long hours of extra studying were spent preparing to pass the entrance exams in order to get into the proper middle school. Young scholars would get up at six in the morning to study before school and then study again after school until midnight. Children became walking encyclopedias by the time they graduated from elementary school! Because so many parents endured great hardships due to their lack of education, they believe that education is the key to future success. Compulsory schooling for all and the abolishment of entrance examinations for primary and secondary schools have certainly removed some of the pressures. But there is naturally a strong desire to obtain a higher education, and competition for entrance to universities is keen.

School life is regimented with uniforms, segregated classes, assemblies, and rules. But there is a great respect and love between students and teachers, and school is not all dull studying. Sports and music are popular activities and some children attend extra classes after school to learn traditional folk dances or practice the ever popular *tae kwon do.* Sometimes referred to as

Korean karate, *tae kwon do* is taught in school as a discipline that develops confidence, health, agility, and poise. This art of self-defense has been a Korean sport since the third century A.D., and now there are international rules and competitions. It is unusual in that both defense and attack can be made freely from any direction using various parts of the body.

In spite of their busy days at school, children always have time for a game of *chegi* or *yut*, to spin homemade tops or fly a kite. *Chegi* is a game of skill that can be played anywhere there is a group of boys, an old coin with a square hole in it, and a piece of thin paper. The paper is wrapped around the coin with the corners drawn through the hole and shredded to make a tassel. The result is something like a badminton shuttlecock, and the boys kick it into the air with the side of a foot as many times as they can.

Yut is one of Korea's oldest games, having been played ever since the ninth century, especially during the Lunar New Year holidays. It is played with four short wooden sticks that each have a flat side and a round side. They are tossed into the air to see how they land. The number of round sides up determines the number of moves around the *yut* board. Capturing the opponent's pawn or taking short cuts on the board makes the game more interesting.

Flying bamboo-and-paper kites is a favorite pastime in the winter months. If the strings are strengthened by coating them with powdered glass, a mock battle can be held, with the winner being the one who most skillfully maneuvers his kite string to cut through his opponent's. On the last day of the first moon of the year, children write the names of evil things or diseases on their kites and then let them fly away. Television and sophisticated space-age toys are available, but simple homemade toys are widely seen, especially in rural areas. A wooden top or toy whittled by grandfather or a homemade doll is treasured indeed.

Holidays bring lots of excitement, and the Lunar New Year is extra special. It lasts until the fifteenth day of the first moon, and every day brings its special customs and superstitions. New Year's Day is awaited with great anticipation. Holiday food is prepared and new clothes for everyone in the family are gotten ready. Peddlers call out all night selling baskets to be hung up over the door the next day for good luck. Children try to stay awake until morning in fear that if they fall asleep their eyebrows will turn white!

Everyone rises early on New Year's Day to honor the family's ancestors. The food is laid out and the ceremony begins. Under the solemn direction of the oldest man of the house, the wine is poured, the food is offered, and everyone bows to the ancestors. After a merry breakfast, the children dressed in their new clothes make a special deep bow, all the way to the floor, to their parents, and then spend the day visiting and honoring other relatives.

On the first night of the New Year a ghost comes down from heaven looking for a shoe that fits. Of course the person whose shoe is stolen will have bad luck all year. So everyone hides his shoes indoors, hangs a straw rope across the door to keep out the ghost, and goes to bed very early. The next days are filled with kite flying and games like *yut*, and the girls play see-saw. When all else fails, there is usually a grandparent willing to tell a story.

January 15 according to the lunar calendar is considered important because it is the day of the first full moon of the year. People crack various kinds of nuts to exorcise harmful spirits, and in the evening, neighboring villages compete in different traditional games under the moonlight. Tradition has it that the winning village will be blessed with bumper crops.

Stories and songs are a wonderful part of growing up. Surely every Korean child knows this song from the Silla dynasty, believed to be the oldest folk song in Korea:

Blue bird, blue bird, lovely blue bird,
Do not disturb flow' ring bean plant.
If the flow'r falls no bean will grow.
Jelly maker'll go home in tears.

Schoolchildren wait for the days when their teacher is late or absent so they can spend some delightfully unexpected time singing and telling stories. Gathered around a fire pot on a winter evening or sitting on a straw mat in a shady corner of the courtyard on a hot summer day, grandparents tell their grandchildren stories that they learned from their own grandparents. Even farmers enjoy taking a break from their labors in the fields to share stories full of earthy, ribald humor. There are tales of tigers, fierce and hungry and foolish; stories of why frogs croak when it rains or how the sun and moon and stars got into the sky; stories of spirits who can turn themselves into wild berries; and tales of history and Confucian ethics.

Imagine that the snow is falling gently on the roof and grandmother is roasting chestnuts for the children on a small charcoal brazier. Then grandfather says, "Remember the story about the hungry old tiger? Well, one winter day, just like this, that old tiger was especially hungry and very angry at having been tricked when he happened to see a little rabbit sitting on the riverbank eating some vegetables. The tiger ground his teeth and roared, 'This time I am going to eat you up for sure!'

"But the little rabbit just smiled and said, 'Look, I have been catching fish with my tail. They really are delicious.'

"The hungry tiger thought to himself that surely he could do that even better than the rabbit. And how he loved to eat fish! So he asked the rabbit to show him how to do it.

"'Well it isn't very easy,' said the rabbit, 'but if you just hang your tail in the water very quietly, and close your eyes, I will go and chase the fish in your direction.'

"So the rabbit hopped about on the bank pretending to chase the fish down to the tiger. Meanwhile the day got colder and colder.

"'The fish will be biting any minute, Mr. Tiger,' called the rabbit, as he hopped away.

"The tiger began to feel something heavy on his tail. 'Oh, good,' he thought. 'I must be catching a lot of fish with my tail.' And he waited into the night to be sure he had caught enough for a real feast.

"But when he tried to pull his tail out of the river he couldn't move. It was frozen fast in the ice.

"The tiger groaned, 'Oh, I have been tricked again.' But it was too late.

"In the morning the villagers found him stuck in the ice. And that old tiger will never eat another rabbit!"

The children fall asleep, sleepy and satisfied. They dream about the clever rabbit and the tiger's frozen tail and smile.

The wondrous time of childhood. What could be more fun than riding a go-kart and trading baseball cards!

In the bamboo forest grows a friendship that in later years will treasure the memories of childhood. Bamboo has been a popular theme in Korean poetry and painting because it remains straight and evergreen throughout the changing seasons.

Following page: A few schoolboys still spin colorful old-fashioned wooden tops in a game of the past. Playing coin-operated television games at neighborhood street corners has become more popular among children of today's fast-changing society.

Coca-Cola
윈써식품
우진정육

Middle-school children dressed in their school uniforms line up to begin the new school day. The entire student body assembles to bow to their teachers and listen to the principal's daily address and announcements. After the assembly the children march off to class to the tune of a Sousa march and begin the first lesson of the day.

Many schools still place boys and girls in separate classrooms according to the traditional belief that boys and girls should not sit together after the age of seven.

The school bell brings laughter to the classroom. Nothing matches the magic of recess for the little girls so eager to share their stories.

In spite of limited opportunities for education during the old kingdoms and the "deintellectualization" of Koreans during the Japanese occupation, the Korean people's constant striving for education has brought about many changes. Compulsory education combined with a high regard for the importance of learning is responsible for one of the highest literacy rates in the world. King Sejong helped advance Korean learning through his development of *han'gul*, the twenty-four-letter Korean alphabet. In use now for five hundred years, *han'gul* is easily learned.

The sound of bamboo flutes echoes in the empty hallway as a few students practice after school. Reflected in this pair of bright brown eyes are the desire to learn and the determination to carry on the old traditions.

The roads the ancestors traveled have been rough and their journeys sometimes broken, but it is the confident spirit of today's generation that holds the key to Korean destiny. These young people may inherit the task of unifying the divided peninsula for its everlasting peace and harmony.

China
Yalu R.
Pyongyang
North Korea
SEA OF JAPAN
(East Sea)
DMZ
38°
Panmunjon
Chunchon
Han R.
Inchon
SEOUL
Kanghwa Bay
Suwon
Wonju
T'AEBAEK MTS.
Mt. T'aebaek
Chongju
Ullung Is.
YELLOW SEA
SOBAEK MTS.
Taejon
36°
Pohang
Kunsan
Taegu
Chonju
Kyongju
Ulsan
Pusan
Masan
Kwangju
Mokpo
Yosu
34°
KOREA STRAIT
EAST CHINA SEA
(South Sea)
Cheju City
Cheju Is.
Japan
0
50
100 miles
124°
126°
128°
130°

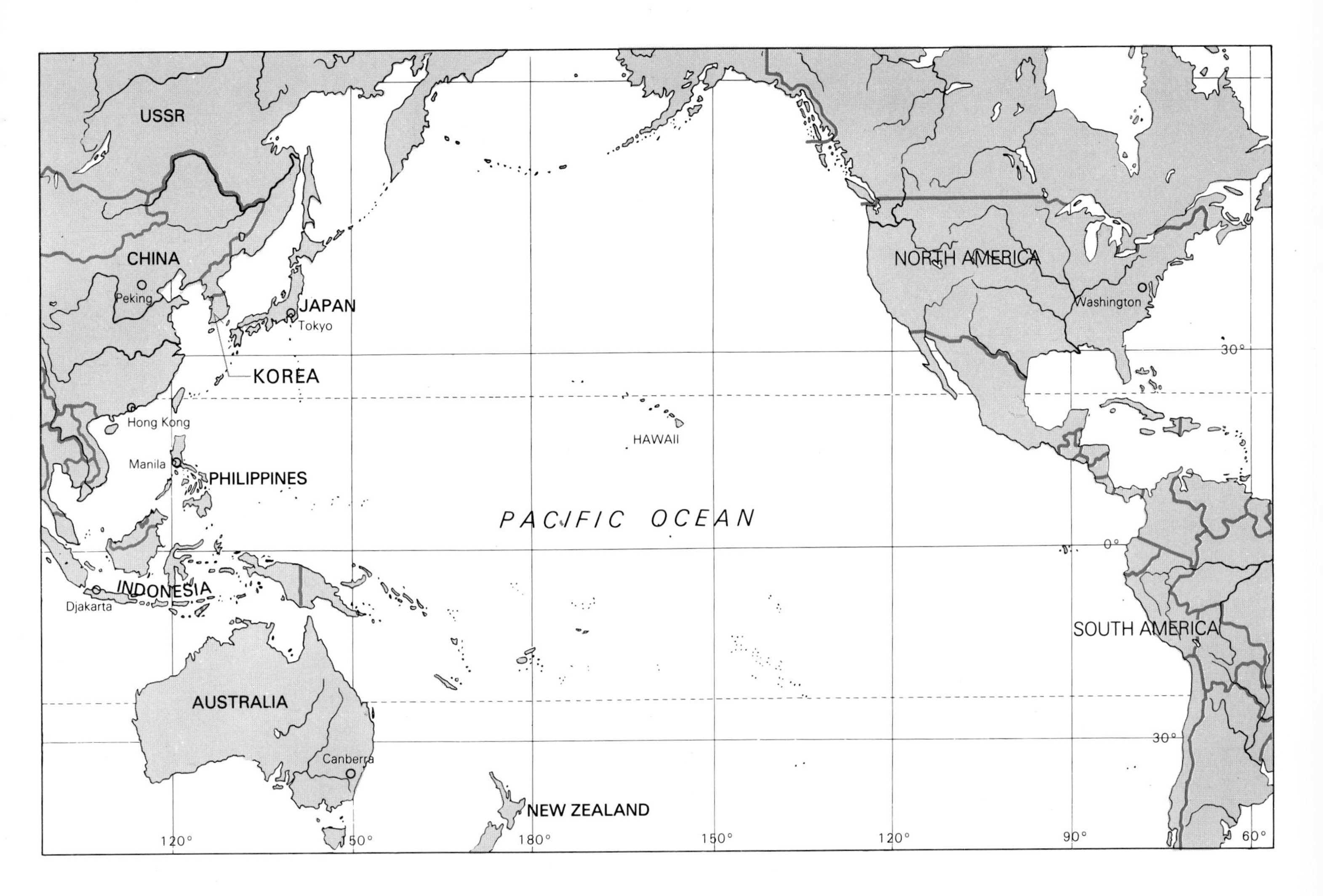

Korea and the Pacific Region

Throughout the centuries, Korea's geographical location has brought the peninsula into close contact with its two powerful neighbors, China to the west and Japan to the east. This has been to Korea's benefit culturally. But it has also made Korea an object of invasion, conquest, and brutal exploitation. Yet the Korean people have retained their unique character. South Koreans today are well aware of the strategic role their nation continues to play in East Asia and the Pacific region. Fiercely independent, they are determined to keep Korea strong, vigilant, and economically sound.

Official name: Republic of Korea. *Population (1979 est.):* 37,600,000. *Area:* 38,031 sq. mi. *Capital:* Seoul. *Chief ports:* Pusan, Inchon. *Industries:* Clothing, textiles, electronic equipment, shipbuilding, processed foods, concrete, plywood, steel, glass, chemicals, rubber, oil products. *Crops:* Rice, wheat, barley, soybeans, tobacco, ginseng. *Minerals:* Iron and copper ore, tungsten, coal, graphite. *Gross national product (1979):* $46.08 billion.

SOURCES

The poems on pages 10, 18–19, 46, 74–76, 150–51, and 166 of this book were taken from *The Bamboo Grove: An Introduction to Sijo*, edited and translated by Richard Rutt (Berkeley: University of California Press, 1971): "Let my house be morning mists" (no. 172); "When I quietly close my eyes, I see" (no. 258); "The Great String of the Black Lute sounds" (no. 103); "The day-star's set, the larks are in the sky" (no. 159); "At the end of ten years' work" (no. 154); and "The long rains have stopped awhile" (no. 193). The poems on pages 99, 112–13, and 132–33 were taken from *Poetry and Music of the Classic Age*, by Tae Hung Ha, Korean Cultural Series, vol. 4 (Seoul: Yonsei University Press, 1958): "Happy Country Life" (p. 41); "Maple Rock in Autumn" (p. 25); and "The Boat Has Sailed with My Love" (p. 47). All poems are used with permission of the publishers.